Poems of John Keats

POEMS OF

JOHN KEATS

Selected by Stanley Kunitz

WOODCUTS BY

JACQUES HNIZDOVSKY

———

Thomas Y. Crowell Company · New York

Contents

Poems of John Keats

The Burning Fountain

... the pure spirit shall flow
Back to the burning fountain whence it came ...
—PERCY BYSSHE SHELLEY, *Adonais*

To CONSIDER the life of John Keats is to recall his own prophetic comment: "A Man's life of any worth is a continual allegory." He belongs almost as much to legend as he does to the history of literature. More than anybody else he is responsible for the modern image of the Romantic poet. It is not an image that he inherited; it is, rather, an image that he created in his works and days, out of the ardent beauty of his character, the "fine excess" of his imagination, the cruel brevity of his span. Modern readers do not need to be told to admire John Keats: whether they know it or not, he has already entered into their dreams, he is a portion of their hopes, he lives in their desires. As Shelley wrote in "Adonais," his elegy on the death of Keats: "He is a presence to be felt and known in darkness and in light. . . . He is a portion of the loveliness which once he made more lovely."

The circumstances of Keats's birth on the 31st of October, 1795, can scarcely be termed propitious for the production of an immortal, but genius has a way of striking in unlikely places. In this case the location was the Swan and Hoop Livery Stables at 24 Moorfields Pavement Row, close to what was then the northern limits of London. John was the first child of a young couple who kept horses for hire. When John was eight, his father was killed by a fall from a horse. Two months later the widow entered into an unhappy and short-lived second marriage. John, together with his two younger brothers George and Tom and his baby sister Fanny, was surrendered to the care of his maternal grandmother. The death of his mother, presumably of consumption, in 1810 left Keats at fourteen the eldest son in a family of orphans, soon to be bereft of their last protector. When their grandmother died in 1814, the inheritance that would have kept them fairly comfortable was entrusted to a tea merchant, Richard Abbey, who turned out to be niggardly and dishonest, with the result that Keats was never to be free from anxiety about money. From the vantage-point of another century it is some consolation to reflect that the Keats children—all except sweet-natured Tom, who died at nineteen—surmounted their vicissitudes and fulfilled their lives as free-ranging and courageous spirits. George, who was especially close to John, emigrated to America as soon as he achieved manhood and, after many trials, became a prosperous merchant in Louisville. Fanny went off to Spain to live with her cultivated Spanish husband. John traveled to Rome, at twenty-five, to die in agony and to be reborn in the memory of men.

Keats did not go to college. His entire schooling consisted of eight years at a small academy in the country village of Enfield, some ten miles from London. Shortly before his sixteenth birthday he was taken out of school by his guardian, Abbey, and apprenticed to a surgeon and apothecary, Thomas Hammond, in nearby Edmonton. To be a surgeon at that time was to be something less than a physician, of whom professional study at a university was required: the surgeon performed practical services, such as setting bones and pulling teeth, and administered drugs and advice in simple cases. Keats completed his medical training at Guy's Hospital in the slums of London, just south of London Bridge. The dressing of infected wounds was one of his principal activities. In July,

1816, he received his license to practice as apothecary and surgeon as soon as he became twenty-one. By the date of his birthday next autumn, he had made a different kind of commitment. If the world, in consequence, lost an indifferent surgeon, it gained one of the most pure and eloquent of the English poets.

Now the wheel of life—and of death—began to turn for him at a dizzying and frightful speed. Though his creative flight had scarcely begun, he had less than five years left in which to draw breath on this planet, actually only three years of productivity, after which he would be far too exhausted by illness to task himself further.

His first verses were imitative and fumbling, but by the end of 1816 he had written one of the greatest English sonnets and announced the seriousness of his ambition by pushing to conclusion, in spite of directional uncertainties, two longish discursive poems ("I Stood Tip-toe" and "Sleep and Poetry") that speak of nature and of art . . . and of the visionary gleam. The sonnet that far transcended the rest of his early efforts was the offshoot of a memorable night in which Keats and his old school friend, Charles Cowden Clarke, leafed through a borrowed folio edition of George Chapman's seventeenth-century translation of Homer and read the resounding lines aloud to each other with mounting excitement and delight. Keats wrote his sonnet, "On First Looking into Chapman's Homer," within the space of two hours beginning at daybreak. In this same year Keats met several persons whose names are inextricably linked with his: the poet Leigh Hunt, who influenced him with his liberal politics and, for a while, with his soft style; the painter Benjamin Robert Haydon, who walked in the aura of genius diffused by his aggressive enthusiasms; the tender-hearted young artist Joseph Severn, who was destined to witness the ordeal of Keats's end; and the

3

witty and ill-fated versifier John Hamilton Reynolds, whose obscure tombstone on the Isle of Wight is engraved with the telling words: "The Friend of Keats."

[The so-called Keats Circle soon expanded to include Charles Armitage Brown, steadfast, practical, quick-witted, in whose two-family house in Hampstead, Wentworth Place, now a literary shrine, Keats came to live after the death of Tom; Charles Wentworth Dilke, editor and scholar, whose hospitality to the young poet prefigured his life-long loyalty to his memory; John Taylor, blessed among publishers for his taste and for his generosity; and Richard Woodhouse, legal adviser to the publishing firm of Taylor & Hessey, a man of infinite tact and kindness, to whom Keats wrote his famous comment on "the poetical character." Clearly Keats had as great a gift for friendship as for poetry, and no man could have been luckier in his friends. In addition he knew Wordsworth and Shelley, but did not count them among his intimates. After his one chance encounter with Coleridge—on April 11, 1819, on a lane near Highgate, across from Hampstead Heath— the older poet turned to his walking companion and remarked, "There is death in that hand."]

It was Reynolds who wrote memorially of Keats that he was not only "the sincerest Friend—the most lovable associate,— the deepest Listener to the griefs & disappointments of all around him," but that "He had the greatest power of poetry in him, of any one since Shakespeare." Wordsworth, Hunt, and Haydon were the three luminaries celebrated by Keats in his optimistic sonnet beginning, "Great spirits now on earth are sojourning."

The publication of Keats's first volume of *Poems* in the spring of 1817 created no stir whatever, except in the poet's own immediate circle. Indeed, except for the "Chapman's Homer" sonnet, it contained no poem of absolutely first quality; it was

4

easier to spot the echoes of Spenser and of Hunt than to recognize the intimations of original power in the occasional freshness of the natural descriptions, the tentative efforts to evoke a world of classic enchantment, and the earnest dedications to the muse. Undismayed, Keats immediately proceeded to put himself to a test, to "a trial of my Powers of Imagination," by attempting a long poem, the "poetic romance" *Endymion*, in four books of roughly a thousand lines each. The main line of the narrative—by no means a straight line—concerns itself with the story of Endymion, the "brain-sick shepherd-prince" of Mt. Latmos, with whom the moon goddess falls in love. Fevered and perplexed, he is lured by her through "cloudy phantasms" and eventually carried away to eternal life at her side. The poem can be read as a rather circuitous allegory of the poet torn between his quest of ideal perfection and his distracting love for human beauty; but Keats seems to have been less concerned with the development of the theme than with the task of filling 4000 lines. On November 28, 1817, some eight months after starting *Endymion*, he completed his assignment. At the last he was writing more than eighty lines a day on the average. He realized that it was a flawed performance, as a whole, despite the transparent beauty of the opening lines and the splendid choral resonances in Books I and IV; but he was anxious to hurry on to other tasks, now that he had learned what he had to learn.

In his biography of Keats, Sir Sidney Colvin describes him as he appeared to his friends at this time: " 'The character and expression of his features,' it is said, 'would arrest even the casual passenger in the street.' A small, handsome, ardent-looking youth—the stature little over five feet: the figure compact and well-turned, with the neck thrust eagerly forward, carrying a strong and shapely head set off by thickly clustering gold-brown hair: the features powerful, finished and mobile: the mouth rich and wide, with an expression at once combative and sensitive in the extreme: the forehead not high, but broad and strong: the eyebrows nobly arched, and eyes hazel-brown, liquid-flashing, visibly inspired—'an eye that had an inward look, perfectly divine, like a Delphian priestess who saw visions'. . . ."

For a while the three Keats brothers shared lodgings in Hampstead, where they had easy access to the city and yet—particularly for Tom's benefit—could enjoy the open air. With his restless temperament John took off, from time to time, to other parts in search of an ideal working-place. In mid-1818 George left for America with his bride to make his fortune, while John went on a strenuous walking-tour of the Lake District and Scotland with his friend Charles Brown. Returning in August, in weakened physical condition as a result of having over-extended himself in mountain-climbing, he found Tom, four years his junior, desperately ill. In all likelihood he contracted tuberculosis during the next few weeks, while nursing Tom through his fatal illness.

Meanwhile the reviews of his *Endymion*, which had gone to press in the spring, finally appeared. They were brutally unkind. Keats was hurt by their ridicule more than he would admit, but he was by no means crushed. To George he wrote quietly, firmly: "This is a mere matter of the moment—I think I shall be among the English Poets after my death." His even bolder gesture was to begin work on *Hyperion*, which, despite its unfinished state, retains an air of noble grandeur. There had been something boyish and appealing, despite the reviewers, about *Endymion*; the imagination responsible for *Hyperion* has severity and magnitude—it is, above all, manly. Suddenly Keats is in command of an epic voice, in the high Miltonic style.

The idea of a poem on the fall of the Titans, with Apollo the god of light and song as its hero, had occurred to him while he was still grinding away at *Endymion*. In the actual writing he became absorbed in the tragic fate of Hyperion, the older god of the Sun, whom Apollo dethrones. The theme offered certain parallels with Keats's own sense of his plight as a poet of the new age (Apollo) striving to achieve a work of the original imagination, while at the same time stirred by the power and magnitude of his divinely gifted predecessor (Hyperion).

Two cataclysmic events shook Keats at the end of 1818: "poor Tom" died on the first of December; by Christmas, John had fallen wildly in love with Fanny Brawne. As the letters testify, the only love for a woman that could be meaningful, or even possible, for him was a passion that matched in intensity his consuming love for poetry. These two loves were not at peace with each other; on the contrary, they fought for possession of him. He was already agitated by the loss of his brother and beginning to be worried about his own health, specifically about a chronic "sore throat" that he could not shake off. Furthermore, his mind was in a constant fever of creation. We ought not to forget that Keats had just turned twenty-three; Fanny was a young charmer of eighteen.

In the history of English poetry Keats's next year (1819) must be counted among the miracles. In January he wrote "The Eve of St. Agnes" over a period of nine or ten days. April saw the birth, in a single session, of "La Belle Dame sans Merci." The real explosion came in May, when (ignoring lesser poems) three of the finest odes in the language ("Nightingale," "Grecian Urn," and "Melancholy") were completed within fifteen days. During the summer he worked on "Lamia" and "The Fall of Hyperion." The last of the odes, "To Autumn," unique in its music and its majesty, was written on a Sunday in September. Two days later he abandoned his exalted second try at the Hyperion myth, recast in the form of a dream. And that was about it. The rest was a dwindling and a torment.

While his illness secretly attacked him, Keats became increasingly subject to fits of despondency. He was particularly sensitive to the fact that he was living on borrowed money, which he saw little chance of repaying. "I will no longer live upon hopes," he announced, after completing his "Autumn" ode in September, but his resolution to find gainful employment ended in an abortive effort to get some hack writing assignments. He was fatigued in body and in spirit. "My mind is in a tremble," he wrote to Fanny on October 19, "I cannot tell what I am writing."

On the night of February 3, 1820, after riding home to Hampstead, in a state of chill and fever, on top of the coach (where the fare was cheapest), Keats suffered a violent hemorrhage in the lungs. To his friend who ministered to him he called, "Bring me the candle, Brown; and let me see this blood." His next words were not to be forgotten: "I know the color of that blood;—it is arterial blood;—I cannot be deceived in that color;—that drop of blood is my death-warrant; —I must die."

Ten days later he wrote to James Rice: "How astonishingly does the chance of leaving the world impress a sense of its natural beauties on us. Like poor Falstaff, though I do not babble, I think of green fields. I muse with the greatest affection on every flower I have known from my infancy—their shapes and colors are as new to me as if I had just created them with a superhuman fancy—It is because they are connected with the most thoughtless and happiest moments of our Lives —I have seen foreign flowers in hothouses of the most beautiful nature, but I do not care a straw for them. The simple flowers of our spring are what I want to see again."

Keats's extraordinary third volume—the last to be published during his lifetime—appeared in July. The reviews that gradually drifted in were more favorable than the report of sales, but by this time Keats had his mind on other matters. The hemorrhaging had resumed. He was told that he could not survive another winter in England. Thanks to the generosity of his publishers, Keats embarked for Italy, in the company of Joseph Severn, on September 17. After an excruciatingly slow and rough voyage, thwarted by unfavorable winds, the small brig sailed into the Bay of Naples more than a month later. A week's trip to Rome, by hired carriage, proved a far from restful adventure. In Rome, Keats and Severn rented rooms next to the Spanish Steps (No. 26 Piazza di Spagna), now famous as the Keats-Shelley Memorial House. There Keats, who had just passed his twenty-fifth birthday, failed rapidly. In the light of modern knowledge, nothing could have been worse for him than the harrowing flight to a country of strangers, the starvation diet on which he was put, the frequent blood-lettings then prescribed for treatment. No wonder he inquired of his doctor, "How long is this posthumous life of mine to last?" His own knowledge of medicine told him of the hopelessness of his condition. Even his friend prayed that the end would come soon.

Around four in the afternoon of February 23, 1821, in the words of Severn writing to Brown, "the approaches of death came on. 'Severn—I—lift me up—I am dying—I shall die easy—don't be frightened—be firm, and thank God it has come!' I lifted him up in my arms. The phlegm seemed boiling in his throat, and increased until 11, when he gradually sunk into death—so quiet—that I still thought he slept."

Keats was buried in the Protestant Cemetery in Rome. In compliance with his deathbed wishes, no name appears on his tombstone. The words he requested for his epitaph read: "Here lies one whose name was writ in water."

Prefatory Note

THIS VOLUME is designed to serve as an introduction, in fitting and attractive format, to the work of John Keats. The arrangement of the poems, in eight sections, is intended to show the general development of Keats as a poet, while at the same time grouping, as far as possible, those poems that are related to one another in form or in theme. Excerpts from the letters of Keats are distributed throughout the text where they are pertinent. It should be a pleasure to find them among the poems, which they so richly complement and illuminate, much as they did for Keats's friends during his lifetime.

In selecting the poems the aim has been to present Keats at his finest and most enjoyable. No shorter poems have been omitted that appeared to the editor to be of first quality. The most representative of the verse narratives, "The Eve of St. Agnes," is presented complete, as is the first book of *Hyperion*. Aside from "Lamia," which resists abridgment, the rest of the major longer poems can be sampled here in key passages that are calculated to lead, as Keats might say in his Bible-echoing phraseology, "to a large Mansion of Many Apartments."

S. K.

I. Adam's Dream

FROM: I STOOD TIP-TOE

"Places of nestling green for Poets made."
Story of Rimini [Leigh Hunt]

I STOOD tip-toe upon a little hill,
The air was cooling, and so very still,
That the sweet buds which with a modest pride
Pull droopingly, in slanting curve aside,
Their scantly leaved, and finely tapering stems,
Had not yet lost those starry diadems
Caught from the early sobbing of the morn.
The clouds were pure and white as flocks new shorn,
And fresh from the clear brook; sweetly they slept
On the blue fields of heaven, and then there crept
A little noiseless noise among the leaves,
Born of the very sigh that silence heaves:
For not the faintest motion could be seen
Of all the shades that slanted o'er the green.
There was wide wand'ring for the greediest eye,
To peer about upon variety;
Far round the horizon's crystal air to skim,
And trace the dwindled edgings of its brim;
To picture out the quaint, and curious bending
Of a fresh woodland alley, never ending;
Or by the bowery clefts, and leafy shelves,
Guess where the jaunty streams refresh themselves.
I gazed awhile, and felt as light, and free
As though the fanning wings of Mercury
Had play'd upon my heels: I was light-hearted,
And many pleasures to my vision started. . . .

"THE TRUTH OF IMAGINATION"

I am certain of nothing but of the holiness of the Heart's affections and the truth of Imagination—What the imagination seizes as Beauty must be truth—whether it existed before or not—for I have the same Idea of all our Passions as of Love they are all in their sublime, creative of essential Beauty. . . .

The Imagination may be compared to Adam's dream—he awoke and found it truth. I am the more zealous in this affair, because I have never yet been able to perceive how any thing can be known for truth by consequitive reasoning—and yet it must be—Can it be that even the greatest Philosopher ever arrived at his goal without putting aside numerous objections—However it may be, O for a Life of Sensations rather than of Thoughts ! It is 'a Vision in the form of Youth' a Shadow of reality to come. . . .

I scarcely remember counting upon any Happiness—I look not for it if it be not in the present hour—nothing startles me beyond the Moment. The setting sun will always set me to rights—or if a Sparrow come before my Window I take part in its existence and pick about the Gravel.
— To Benjamin Bailey, November 22, 1817.

16

FROM: SLEEP AND POETRY

STOP AND CONSIDER! life is but a day;
A fragile dew-drop on its perilous way
From a tree's summit; a poor Indian's sleep
While his boat hastens to the monstrous steep
Of Montmorenci. Why so sad a moan?
Life is the rose's hope while yet unblown;
The reading of an ever-changing tale;
The light uplifting of a maiden's veil;
A pigeon tumbling in clear summer air;
A laughing school-boy, without grief or care,
Riding the springy branches of an elm.

O for ten years, that I may overwhelm
Myself in poesy; so I may do the deed
That my own soul has to itself decreed. . . .

. . . A drainless shower
Of light is poesy; 'tis the supreme of power;
'Tis might half slumb'ring on its own right arm.
The very archings of her eye-lids charm
A thousand willing agents to obey,
And still she governs with the mildest sway:
But strength alone though of the Muses born
Is like a fallen angel: trees uptorn,
Darkness, and worms, and shrouds, and sepulchres
Delight it; for it feeds upon the burrs,
And thorns of life; forgetting the great end
Of poesy, that it should be a friend
To sooth the cares, and lift the thoughts of man.

17

Yet I rejoice: a myrtle fairer than
E'er grew in Paphos, from the bitter weeds
Lifts its sweet head into the air, and feeds
A silent space with ever sprouting green.
All tenderest birds there find a pleasant screen,
Creep through the shade with jaunty fluttering,
Nibble the little cupped flowers and sing.
Then let us clear away the choking thorns
From round its gentle stem; let the young fawns,
Yeaned in after times, when we are flown,
Find a fresh sward beneath it, overgrown
With simple flowers: let there nothing be
More boisterous than a lover's bended knee;
Nought more ungentle than the placid look
Of one who leans upon a closed book;
Nought more untranquil than the grassy slopes
Between two hills. All hail delightful hopes!
As she was wont, th' imagination
Into most lovely labyrinths will be gone,
And they shall be accounted poet kings
Who simply tell the most heart-easing things.
O may these joys be ripe before I die.

Will not some say that I presumptuously
Have spoken? that from hastening disgrace
'Twere better far to hide my foolish face?
That whining boyhood should with reverence bow
Ere the dread thunderbolt could reach? How!
If I do hide myself, it sure shall be
In the very fane, the light of Poesy:
If I do fall, at least I will be laid
Beneath the silence of a poplar shade;
And over me the grass shall be smooth shaven;

And there shall be a kind memorial graven.
But off Despondence! miserable bane!
They should not know thee, who athirst to gain
A noble end, are thirsty every hour.
What though I am not wealthy in the dower
Of spanning wisdom; though I do not know
The shiftings of the mighty winds that blow
Hither and thither all the changing thoughts
Of man: though no great minist'ring reason sorts
Out the dark mysteries of human souls
To clear conceiving: yet there ever rolls
A vast idea before me, and I glean
Therefrom my liberty; thence too I've seen
The end and aim of Poesy. 'Tis clear
As anything most true; as that the year
Is made of the four seasons—manifest
As a large cross, some old cathedral's crest,
Lifted to the white clouds. Therefore should I
Be but the essence of deformity,
A coward, did my very eye-lids wink
At speaking out what I have dared to think.
Ah! rather let me like a madman run
Over some precipice; let the hot sun
Melt my Dedalian wings, and drive me down
Convuls'd and headlong! Stay! an inward frown
Of conscience bids me be more calm awhile.
An ocean dim, sprinkled with many an isle,
Spreads awfully before me. How much toil!
How many days! what desperate turmoil!
Ere I can have explored its widenesses.
Ah, what a task! upon my bended knees,
I could unsay those—no, impossible!
Impossible!

II. A Test of Invention

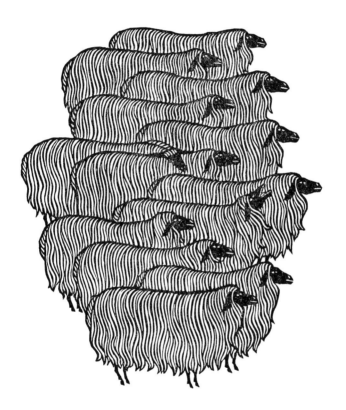

As to what you say about my being a Poet, I can return no answer but by saying that the high idea I have of poetical fame makes me think I see it towering to high above me. At any rate I have no right to talk until Endymion is finished—it will be a test, a trial of my Powers of Imagination and chiefly of my invention which is a rare thing indeed—by which I must make 4000 Lines of one bare circumstance and fill them with Poetry; and when I consider that this is a great task, and that when done it will take me but a dozen paces towards the Temple of Fame—it makes me say—God forbid that I should be without such a task! I have heard [Leigh] Hunt say and may be asked—why endeavour after a long Poem? To which I should answer—Do not the Lovers of Poetry like to have a little Region to wander in where they may pick and choose, and in which the images are so numerous that many are forgotten and found new in a second Reading: which may be food for a Week's stroll in the Summer? Do not they like this better than what they can read before Mrs. Williams comes down stairs? a Morning work at most. Besides a long Poem is a test of Invention which I take to be the Polar Star of Poetry, as Fancy is the Sails, and Imagination the Rudder.

— To Benjamin Bailey, October 8, 1817.

POET AND PUBLIC

I have not the slightest feel of humility towards the Public—or to any thing in existence,—but the eternal Being, the Principle of Beauty,—and the Memory of great Men. . . .

I never wrote one single Line of Poetry with the least Shadow of public thought.

— To J. H. Reynolds, April 9, 1818.

FROM THE PREFACE TO Endymion

The imagination of a boy is healthy, and the mature imagination of a man is healthy; but there is a space of life between, in which the soul

23

is in a ferment, the character undecided, the way of life uncertain, the ambition thick-sighted: thence proceeds mawkishness, and all the thousand bitters which those men I speak of must necessarily taste in going over the following pages.

I hope I have not in too late a day touched the beautiful mythology of Greece, and dulled its brightness: for I wish to try once more, before I bid it farewell.

—*April 10, 1818.*

DARING TO FAIL

[Endymion] *is as good as I had power to make it—by myself— Had I been nervous about its being a perfect piece, & with that view asked advice, & trembled over every page, it would not have been written; for it is not in my nature to fumble—I will write independently. —I have written independently* without Judgment—*I may write independently* & with judgment *hereafter.— The Genius of Poetry must work out its own salvation in a man: It cannot be matured by law & precept, but by sensation & watchfulness in itself— That which is creative must create itself—In Endymion, I leaped headlong into the Sea, and thereby have become better acquainted with the Soundings, the quicksands, & the rocks, than if I had stayed upon the green shore, and piped a silly pipe, and took tea & comfortable advice.—I was never afraid of failure; for I would sooner fail than not be among the greatest.*
— *To J. A. Hessey, October 8, 1818.*

"OF POEMS TO COME"

I am ambitious of doing the world some good: if I should be spared that may be the work of maturer years—in the interval I will assay to reach to as high a summit in Poetry as the nerve bestowed upon me will suffer. The faint conceptions I have of Poems to come brings the blood frequently into my forehead.

— *To Richard Woodhouse, October 27, 1818.*

FROM ENDYMION: A POETIC ROMANCE

Introduction
[Book I]

A THING OF BEAUTY is a joy for ever:
Its loveliness increases; it will never
Pass into nothingness; but still will keep
A bower quiet for us, and a sleep
Full of sweet dreams, and health, and quiet breathing.
Therefore, on every morrow, are we wreathing
A flowery band to bind us to the earth,
Spite of despondence, of the inhuman dearth
Of noble natures, of the gloomy days,
Of all the unhealthy and o'er-darkened ways
Made for our searching: yes, in spite of all,
Some shape of beauty moves away the pall
From our dark spirits. Such the sun, the moon,
Trees old, and young, sprouting a shady boon
For simple sheep; and such are daffodils
With the green world they live in; and clear rills
That for themselves a cooling covert make
'Gainst the hot season; the mid forest brake,
Rich with a sprinkling of fair musk-rose blooms:
And such too is the grandeur of the dooms
We have imagined for the mighty dead;
All lovely tales that we have heard or read:
An endless fountain of immortal drink,
Pouring unto us from the heaven's brink.

Hymn to Pan
[Book I]

"O THOU, whose mighty palace roof doth hang
From jagged trunks, and overshadoweth
Eternal whispers, glooms, the birth, life, death
Of unseen flowers in heavy peacefulness;
Who lov'st to see the hamadryads dress
Their ruffled locks where meeting hazels darken;
And through whole solemn hours dost sit, and hearken
The dreary melody of bedded reeds—
In desolate places, where dank moisture breeds
The pipy hemlock to strange overgrowth;
Bethinking thee, how melancholy loth
Thou wast to lose fair Syrinx—do thou now,
By thy love's milky brow!
By all the trembling mazes that she ran,
Hear us, great Pan!

"O thou, for whose soul-soothing quiet, turtles
Passion their voices cooingly 'mong myrtles,
What time thou wanderest at eventide
Through sunny meadows, that outskirt the side
Of thine enmossed realms: O thou, to whom
Broad leaved fig trees even now foredoom
Their ripen'd fruitage; yellow girted bees
The golden honeycombs; our village leas
Their fairest blossom'd beans and poppied corn;
The chuckling linnet its five young unborn,
To sing for thee; low creeping strawberries
Their summer coolness; pent up butterflies
Their freckled wings; yea, the fresh budding year

All its completions—be quickly near,
By every wind that nods the mountain pine,
O forester divine!

"Thou, to whom every faun and satyr flies
For willing service; whether to surprise
The squatted hare while in half sleeping fit;
Or upward ragged precipices flit
To save poor lambkins from the eagle's maw;
Or by mysterious enticement draw
Bewildered shepherds to their path again;
Or to tread breathless round the frothy main,
And gather up all fancifullest shells
For thee to tumble into Naiads' cells,
And, being hidden, laugh at their out-peeping;
Or to delight thee with fantastic leaping,
The while they pelt each other on the crown
With silvery oak apples, and fir cones brown—
By all the echoes that about thee ring,
Hear us, O satyr king!

"O Hearkener to the loud clapping shears
While ever and anon to his shorn peers
A ram goes bleating: Winder of the horn,
When snouted wild-boars routing tender corn
Anger our huntsmen: Breather round our farms,
To keep off mildews, and all weather harms:
Strange ministrant of undescribed sounds,
That come a swooning over hollow grounds,
And wither drearily on barren moors:
Dread opener of the mysterious doors
Leading to universal knowledge—see,
Great son of Dryope,

The many that are come to pay their vows
With leaves about their brows!

"Be still the unimaginable lodge
For solitary thinkings; such as dodge
Conception to the very bourne of heaven,
Then leave the naked brain: be still the leaven,
That spreading in this dull and clodded earth
Gives it a touch ethereal—a new birth:
Be still a symbol of immensity;
A firmament reflected in a sea;
An element filling the space between;
An unknown—but no more: we humbly screen
With uplift hands our foreheads, lowly bending,
And giving out a shout most heaven rending,
Conjure thee to receive our humble Pæan,
Upon thy Mount Lycean!"

The Triumph of Bacchus
[Book IV]

"BENEATH my palm trees, by the river side,
I sat a weeping: in the whole world wide
There was no one to ask me why I wept,—
        And so I kept
Brimming the water-lily cups with tears
        Cold as my fears.

"Beneath my palm trees, by the river side,
I sat a weeping: what enamour'd bride,
Cheated by shadowy wooer from the clouds,
        But hides and shrouds
Beneath dark palm trees by a river side?

"And as I sat, over the light blue hills
There came a noise of revellers: the rills
Into the wide stream came of purple hue—
     'Twas Bacchus and his crew!
The earnest trumpet spake, and silver thrills
From kissing cymbals made a merry din—
     'Twas Bacchus and his kin!
Like to a moving vintage down they came,
Crown'd with green leaves, and faces all on flame;
All madly dancing through the pleasant valley,
     To scare thee, Melancholy!
O then, O then, thou wast a simple name!
And I forgot thee, as the berried holly
By shepherds is forgotten, when, in June,
Tall chestnuts keep away the sun and moon:—
     I rush'd into the folly!

"Within his car, aloft, young Bacchus stood,
Trifling his ivy-dart, in dancing mood,
     With sidelong laughing;
And little rills of crimson wine imbrued
His plump white arms, and shoulders, enough white
     For Venus' pearly bite:
And near him rode Silenus on his ass,
Pelted with flowers as he on did pass
     Tipsily quaffing.

"Whence came ye, merry Damsels! whence came ye!
So many, and so many, and such glee?
Why have ye left your bowers desolate,
     Your lutes, and gentler fate?—
'We follow Bacchus! Bacchus on the wing,
     A conquering!

Bacchus, young Bacchus! good or ill betide,
We dance before him thorough kingdoms wide:—
Come hither, lady fair, and joined be
　　　To our wild minstrelsy!'

"Whence came ye, jolly Satyrs! whence came ye!
So many, and so many, and such glee?
Why have ye left your forest haunts, why left
　　　Your nuts in oak-tree cleft?—
'For wine, for wine we left our kernel tree;
For wine we left our heath, and yellow brooms,
　　　And cold mushrooms;
For wine we follow Bacchus through the eart 1;
Great God of breathless cups and chirping mirth!—
Come hither, lady fair, and joined be
　　　To our mad minstrelsy!'

"Over wide streams and mountains great we went,
And, save when Bacchus kept his ivy tent,
Onward the tiger and the leopard pants,
　　　With the Asian elephants:
Onward these myriads—with song and dance,
With zebras striped, and sleek Arabians' prance,
Web-footed alligators, crocodiles,
Bearing upon their scaly backs, in files,
Plump infant laughers mimicking the coil
Of seamen, and stout galley-rowers' toil:
With toying oars and silken sails they glide,
　　　Nor care for wind and tide.

"Mounted on panthers' furs and lions' manes,
From rear to van they scour about the plains;
A three days' journey in a moment done:

And always, at the rising of the sun,
About the wilds they hunt with spear and horn,
　　On spleenful unicorn.

"I saw Osirian Egypt kneel adown
　　Before the vine-wreath crown!
I saw parch'd Abyssinia rouse and sing
　　To the silver cymbals' ring!
I saw the whelming vintage hotly pierce
　　Old Tartary the fierce!
The kings of Inde their jewel-sceptres vail,
And from their treasures scatter pearled hail;
Great Brahma from his mystic heaven groans,
　　And all his priesthood moans;
Before young Bacchus' eye-wink turning pale.—
Into these regions came I following him,
Sick hearted, weary—so I took a whim
To stray away into these forests drear
　　Alone, without a peer:
And I have told thee all thou mayest hear."

I find that I cannot exist without poetry—without eternal poetry—half the day will not do—the whole of it—I began with a little, but habit has made me a Leviathan.

　　　　　　　—*To J. H. Reynolds, April 18, 1817.*

III. Sonnets 1816–1818

Memory should not be called knowledge—Many have original Minds who do not think it—they are led away by Custom—Now it appears to me that almost any Man may like the Spider spin from his own inwards his own airy Citadel—the points of leaves and twigs on which the Spider begins her work are few and she fills the Air with a beautiful circuiting: man should be content with as few points to tip with the fine Webb of his Soul and weave a tapestry empyrean—full of Symbols for his spiritual eye, of softness for his spiritual touch, of space for his wandering, of distinctness for his Luxury—But the Minds of Mortals are so different and bent on such diverse Journeys that it may at first appear impossible for any common taste and fellowship to exist between two or three under these suppositions—It is however quite the contrary—Minds would leave each other in contrary directions, traverse each other in Numberless points, and all last greet each other at the Journey's end— An old Man and a child would talk together and the old Man be led on his Path, and the child left thinking—Man should not dispute or assert but whisper results to his neighbour, and thus by every germ of Spirit sucking the Sap from mould ethereal every human might become great, and Humanity instead of being a wide heath of Furse and Briars with here and there a remote Oak or Pine, would become a grand democracy of Forest Trees.

—To J. H. Reynolds, February 19, 1818

MUCH have I travell'd in the realms of gold,
   And many goodly states and kingdoms seen;
   Round many western islands have I been
Which bards in fealty to Apollo hold.
Oft of one wide expanse had I been told
   That deep-brow'd Homer ruled as his demesne;
   Yet did I never breathe its pure serene
Till I heard Chapman speak out loud and bold:
Then felt I like some watcher of the skies
   When a new planet swims into his ken;
Or like stout Cortez when with eagle eyes
   He star'd at the Pacific—and all his men
Look'd at each other with a wild surmise—
   Silent, upon a peak in Darien.

GREAT SPIRITS NOW ON EARTH
ARE SOJOURNING

GREAT SPIRITS now on earth are sojourning;
  He of the cloud, the cataract, the lake,
  Who on Helvellyn's summit, wide awake,
Catches his freshness from Archangel's wing:
He of the rose, the violet, the spring,
  The social smile, the chain for Freedom's sake:
  And lo!—whose stedfastness would never take
A meaner sound than Raphael's whispering.
And other spirits there are standing apart
  Upon the forehead of the age to come;
These, these will give the world another heart,
  And other pulses. Hear ye not the hum
Of mighty workings?——
  Listen awhile ye nations, and be dumb.

KEEN FITFUL GUSTS

KEEN, FITFUL GUSTS are whisp'ring here and there
  Among the bushes half leafless, and dry;
  The stars look very cold about the sky,
And I have many miles on foot to fare.
Yet feel I little of the cool bleak air,
  Or of the dead leaves rustling drearily,
  Or of those silver lamps that burn on high,
Or of the distance from home's pleasant lair:
For I am brimfull of the friendliness
  That in a little cottage I have found;
Of fair-hair'd Milton's eloquent distress,
  And all his love for gentle Lycid drown'd;
Of lovely Laura in her light green dress,
  And faithful Petrarch gloriously crown'd.

ON THE GRASSHOPPER AND CRICKET

THE POETRY OF EARTH is never dead:
   When all the birds are faint with the hot sun,
   And hide in cooling trees, a voice will run
From hedge to hedge about the new-mown mead;
That is the Grasshopper's—he takes the lead
   In summer luxury,—he has never done
   With his delights; for when tired out with fun
He rests at ease beneath some pleasant weed.
The poetry of earth is ceasing never:
   On a lone winter evening, when the frost
      Has wrought a silence, from the stove there shrills
The Cricket's song, in warmth increasing ever,
   And seems to one in drowsiness half lost,
      The Grasshopper's among some grassy hills.

ON SEEING THE ELGIN MARBLES
FOR THE FIRST TIME

MY SPIRIT is too weak; mortality
  Weighs heavily on me like unwilling sleep,
  And each imagin'd pinnacle and steep
Of godlike hardship tells me I must die
Like a sick eagle looking at the sky.
  Yet 'tis a gentle luxury to weep,
  That I have not the cloudy winds to keep
Fresh for the opening of the morning's eye.
Such dim-conceived glories of the brain
  Bring round the heart an undescribable feud;
So do these wonders a most dizzy pain,
  That mingles Grecian grandeur with the rude
Wasting of old Time—with a billowy main,
  A sun, a shadow of a magnitude.

ON THE SEA

IT KEEPS eternal whisperings around
    Desolate shores, and with its mighty swell
    Gluts twice ten thousand Caverns, till the spell
Of Hecate leaves them their old shadowy sound.
Often 'tis in such gentle temper found,
    That scarcely will the very smallest shell
    Be mov'd for days from where it sometime fell,
When last the winds of Heaven were unbound.
Oh ye! who have your eye-balls vex'd and tir'd,
    Feast them upon the wideness of the Sea;
        Oh ye! whose ears are dinn'd with uproar rude,
        Or fed too much with cloying melody—
        Sit ye near some old Cavern's Mouth, and brood
Until ye start, as if the sea-nymphs quir'd!

ON SITTING DOWN TO READ *KING LEAR*
ONCE AGAIN

O GOLDEN-TONGUED Romance with serene lute!
   Fair plumed Syren! Queen of far away!
   Leave melodizing on this wintry day,
Shut up thine olden pages, and be mute:
Adieu! for, once again, the fierce dispute,
     Betwixt damnation and impassion'd clay
     Must I burn through; once more humbly assay
The bitter-sweet of this Shakespearian fruit.
Chief Poet! and ye clouds of Albion,
     Begetters of our deep eternal theme,
When through the old oak forest I am gone,
     Let me not wander in a barren dream,
But when I am consumed in the fire,
Give me new Phœnix wings to fly at my desire.

WHEN I HAVE FEARS

WHEN I HAVE FEARS that I may cease to be
 Before my pen has glean'd my teeming brain,
Before high-piled books, in charact'ry
 Hold like rich garners the full-ripen'd grain;
When I behold, upon the night's starr'd face,
 Huge cloudy symbols of a high romance,
And think that I may never live to trace
 Their shadows, with the magic hand of chance;
And when I feel, fair creature of an hour,
 That I shall never look upon thee more,
Never have relish in the faery power
 Of unreflecting love!—then on the shore
Of the wide world I stand alone, and think
Till Love and Fame to nothingness do sink.

WHAT THE THRUSH SAID

Lines from a Letter to John Hamilton Reynolds

O THOU whose face hath felt the Winter's wind,
    Whose eye has seen the snow-clouds hung in mist,
    And the black elm tops 'mong the freezing stars,
    To thee the spring will be a harvest-time.
O thou whose only book has been the light
    Of supreme darkness, which thou feddest on
    Night after night, when Phœbus was away!
    To thee the Spring shall be a triple morn.
O fret not after knowledge—I have none,
    And yet my song comes native with the warmth.
O fret not after knowledge—I have none,
    And yet the Evening listens. He who saddens
At thought of idleness cannot be idle,
And he's awake who thinks himself asleep.

THE HUMAN SEASONS

FOUR SEASONS fill the measure of the year;
    There are four seasons in the mind of man:
He has his lusty Spring, when fancy clear
    Takes in all beauty with an easy span:
He has his Summer, when luxuriously
    Spring's honied cud of youthful thought he loves
To ruminate, and by such dreaming nigh
    Is nearest unto heaven: quiet coves
His soul has in its Autumn, when his wings
    He furleth close; contented so to look
On mists in idleness—to let fair things
    Pass by unheeded as a threshold brook.
He has his Winter too of pale misfeature,
Or else he would forego his mortal nature.

IV. Odes

I.

*Brown & Dilke walked with me & back from the Christmas panto-
mime. I had not a dispute but a disquisition with Dilke, on various
subjects; several things dovetailed in my mind, & at once it struck me,
what quality went to form a Man of Achievement especially in Literature & which Shakespeare possessed so enormously—I mean* Negative
Capability, *that is when man is capable of being in uncertainties,
Mysteries, doubts, without any irritable reaching after fact & reason—
Coleridge, for instance, would let go by a fine isolated verisimilitude
caught from the Penetralium of mystery, from being incapable of re-
maining content with half knowledge.*

—To George and Tom Keats, December, 1817.

2.

*As to the poetical Character itself, (I mean that sort of which, if I
am any thing, I am a Member; that sort distinguished from the words-
worthian or egotistical sublime; which is a thing per se and stands
alone) it is not itself—it has no self—it is every thing and nothing—It
has no character—it enjoys light and shade; it lives in gusto, be it foul
or fair, high or low, rich or poor, mean or elevated—It has as much
delight in conceiving an Iago as an Imogen. What shocks the virtuous
philosopher, delights the chameleon Poet. It does no harm from its
relish of the dark side of things any more than from its taste for the
bright one; because they both end in speculation. A Poet is the most
unpoetical of any thing in existence; because he has no Identity—he is
continually in for—and filling some other Body—The Sun, the Moon,
the Sea and Men and Women who are creatures of impulse are poetical
and have about them an unchangeable attribute—the poet has none; no
identity—he is certainly the most unpoetical of all God's Creatures. If
then he has no self, and if I am a Poet, where is the Wonder that I
should say I would write no more? Might I not at that very instant*

have been cogitating on the Characters of Saturn and Ops? It is a wretched thing to confess; but it a very fact that not one word I ever utter can be taken for granted as an opinion growing out of my identical nature—how can it, when I have no nature? When I am in a room with People if I ever am free from speculating on creations of my own brain, then not myself goes home to myself: but the identity of every one in the room begins to press upon me that, I am in a very little time annihilated —not only among Men; it would be the same in a Nursery of children.
— To Richard Woodhouse, October 27, 1818.

FRAGMENT OF AN ODE TO MAIA,
WRITTEN ON MAY DAY, 1818

MOTHER OF HERMES! and still youthful Maia!
      May I sing to thee
As thou wast hymned on the shores of Baiæ?
      Or may I woo thee
In earlier Sicilian? or thy smiles
Seek as they once were sought, in Grecian isles,
By bards who died content on pleasant sward,
  Leaving great verse unto a little clan?
O, give me their old vigour, and unheard
  Save of the quiet primrose, and the span
      Of heaven and few ears,
Rounded by thee, my song should die away
      Content as theirs,
Rich in the simple worship of a day.

ODE

[Written on the blank page before Beaumont and Fletcher's Tragi-Comedy "The Fair Maid of the Inn."]

BARDS OF PASSION and of Mirth,
Ye have left your souls on earth!
Have ye souls in heaven too,
Double-lived in regions new?
Yes, and those of heaven commune
With the spheres of sun and moon;
With the noise of fountains wond'rous,
And the parle of voices thund'rous;
With the whisper of heaven's trees
And one another, in soft ease
Seated on Elysian lawns
Brows'd by none but Dian's fawns;
Underneath large blue-bells tented,
Where the daisies are rose-scented,
And the rose herself has got
Perfume which on earth is not;
Where the nightingale doth sing
Not a senseless, tranced thing,
But divine melodious truth;
Philosophic numbers smooth;
Tales and golden histories
Of heaven and its mysteries.

Thus ye live on high, and then
On the earth ye live again;
And the souls ye left behind you
Teach us, here, the way to find you,
Where your other souls are joying,

Never slumber'd, never cloying.
Here, your earth-born souls still speak
To mortals, of their little week;
Of their sorrows and delights;
Of their passions and their spites;
Of their glory and their shame;
What doth strengthen and what maim.
Thus ye teach us, every day,
Wisdom, though fled far away.

Bards of Passion and of Mirth,
Ye have left your souls on earth!
Ye have souls in heaven too,
Double-lived in regions new!

ODE TO A NIGHTINGALE

I

My heart aches, and a drowsy numbness pains
  My sense, as though of hemlock I had drunk,
Or emptied some dull opiate to the drains
  One minute past, and Lethe-wards had sunk:
'Tis not through envy of thy happy lot,
  But being too happy in thine happiness,—
    That thou, light-winged Dryad of the trees,
      In some melodious plot
  Of beechen green, and shadows numberless,
    Singest of summer in full-throated ease.

II

O, for a draught of vintage! that hath been
  Cool'd a long age in the deep-delved earth,
Tasting of Flora and the country green,
  Dance, and Provençal song, and sunburnt mirth!
O for a beaker full of the warm South,
  Full of the true, the blushful Hippocrene,
    With beaded bubbles winking at the brim,
      And purple-stained mouth;
    That I might drink, and leave the world unseen,
    And with thee fade away into the forest dim:

III

Fade far away, dissolve, and quite forget
  What thou among the leaves hast never known,
The weariness, the fever, and the fret
  Here, where men sit and hear each other groan;
Where palsy shakes a few, sad, last gray hairs,

Where youth grows pale, and spectre-thin, and dies;
  Where but to think is to be full of sorrow
    And leaden-eyed despairs,
  Where Beauty cannot keep her lustrous eyes,
    Or new Love pine at them beyond to-morrow.

IV

Away! away! for I will fly to thee.
  Not charioted by Bacchus and his pards,
But on the viewless wings of Poesy,
  Though the dull brain perplexes and retards:
Already with thee! tender is the night,
  And haply the Queen-Moon is on her throne,
    Cluster'd around by all her starry Fays;
      But here there is no light,
  Save what from heaven is with the breezes blown
    Through verdurous glooms and winding mossy ways.

V

I cannot see what flowers are at my feet,
  Nor what soft incense hangs upon the boughs,
But, in embalmed darkness, guess each sweet
  Wherewith the seasonable month endows
The grass, the thicket, and the fruit-tree wild;
  White hawthorn, and the pastoral eglantine;
    Fast fading violets cover'd up in leaves;
      And mid-May's eldest child,
  The coming musk-rose, full of dewy wine,
    The murmurous haunt of flies on summer eves.

VI

Darkling I listen; and, for many a time
  I have been half in love with easeful Death,

Call'd him soft names in many a mused rhyme,
  To take into the air my quiet breath;
Now more than ever seems it rich to die,
  To cease upon the midnight with no pain,
    While thou art pouring forth thy soul abroad
      In such an ecstasy!
  Still wouldst thou sing, and I have ears in vain—
    To thy high requiem become a sod.

VII

Thou wast not born for death, immortal Bird!
  No hungry generations tread thee down;
The voice I hear this passing night was heard
  In ancient days by emperor and clown:
Perhaps the self-same song that found a path
  Through the sad heart of Ruth, when, sick for home,
    She stood in tears amid the alien corn;
      The same that oft-times hath
  Charm'd magic casements, opening on the foam
  Of perilous seas, in faery lands forlorn.

VIII

Forlorn! the very word is like a bell
  To toll me back from thee to my sole self!
Adieu! the fancy cannot cheat so well
  As she is fam'd to do, deceiving elf.
Adieu! adieu! thy plaintive anthem fades
  Past the near meadows, over the still stream,
    Up the hill-side; and now 'tis buried deep
      In the next valley-glades:
  Was it a vision, or a waking dream,
  Fled is that music:—Do I wake or sleep?

ODE ON A GRECIAN URN

I

THOU STILL unravish'd bride of quietness,
  Thou foster-child of silence and slow time,
Sylvan historian, who canst thus express
  A flowery tale more sweetly than our rhyme:
What leaf-fring'd legend haunts about thy shape
  Of deities or mortals, or of both,
    In Tempe or the dales of Arcady?
What men or gods are these? What maidens loth?
What mad pursuit? What struggle to escape?
    What pipes and timbrels? What wild ecstasy?

II

Heard melodies are sweet, but those unheard
  Are sweeter; therefore, ye soft pipes, play on;
Not to the sensual ear, but, more endear'd,
  Pipe to the spirit ditties of no tone:
Fair youth, beneath the trees, thou canst not leave
  Thy song, nor ever can those trees be bare;
    Bold Lover, never, never canst thou kiss,
Though winning near the goal—yet, do not grieve;
    She cannot fade, though thou hast not thy bliss,
  For ever wilt thou love, and she be fair!

III

Ah, happy, happy boughs! that cannot shed
  Your leaves, nor ever bid the Spring adieu;
And, happy melodist, unwearied,
  For ever piping songs for ever new;

More happy love! more happy, happy love!
  For ever warm and still to be enjoy'd,
    For ever panting, and for ever young;
All breathing human passion far above,
  That leaves a heart high-sorrowful and cloy'd,
    A burning forehead, and a parching tongue.

IV

Who are these coming to the sacrifice?
  To what green altar, O mysterious priest,
Lead'st thou that heifer lowing at the skies,
  And all her silken flanks with garlands drest?
What little town by river or sea shore,
  Or mountain-built with peaceful citadel,
    Is emptied of this folk, this pious morn?
And, little town, thy streets for evermore
  Will silent be; and not a soul to tell
    Why thou art desolate, can e'er return.

V

O Attic shape! Fair attitude! with brede
  Of marble men and maidens overwrought,
With forest branches and the trodden weed;
  Thou, silent form, dost tease us out of thought
As doth eternity: Cold Pastoral!
  When old age shall this generation waste,
    Thou shalt remain, in midst of other woe
  Than ours, a friend to man, to whom thou say'st
"Beauty is truth, truth beauty,"—that is all
    Ye know on earth, and all ye need to know.

ODE ON MELANCHOLY

I

No, no, go not to Lethe, neither twist
  Wolf's-bane, tight-rooted, for its poisonous wine:
Nor suffer thy pale forehead to be kiss'd
  By nightshade, ruby grape of Proserpine;
Make not your rosary of yew-berries,
  Nor let the beetle, nor the death-moth be
  Your mournful Psyche, nor the downy owl
A partner in your sorrow's mysteries;
  For shade to shade will come too drowsily,
    And drown the wakeful anguish of the soul.

II

But when the melancholy fit shall fall
  Sudden from heaven like a weeping cloud,
That fosters the droop-headed flowers all,
  And hides the green hill in an April shroud;
Then glut thy sorrow on a morning rose,
  Or on the rainbow of the salt sand-wave,
  Or on the wealth of globed peonies;
Or if thy mistress some rich anger shows,
  Emprison her soft hand, and let her rave,
    And feed deep, deep upon her peerless eyes.

III

She dwells with Beauty—Beauty that must die;
  And Joy, whose hand is ever at his lips
Bidding adieu; and aching Pleasure nigh,
  Turning to Poison while the bee-mouth sips:

Ay, in the very temple of Delight
   Veil'd Melancholy has her sovran shrine,
      Though seen of none save him whose strenuous
         tongue
   Can burst Joy's grape against his palate fine;
His soul shall taste the sadness of her might,
      And be among her cloudy trophies hung.

TO AUTUMN

I

Season of mists and mellow fruitfulness,
  Close bosom-friend of the maturing sun;
Conspiring with him how to load and bless
    With fruit the vines that round the thatch-eves run;
To bend with apples the moss'd cottage-trees,
  And fill all fruit with ripeness to the core;
    To swell the gourd, and plump the hazel shells
  With a sweet kernel; to set budding more,
And still more, later flowers for the bees,
Until they think warm days will never cease,
    For Summer has o'er-brimm'd their clammy cells.

II

Who hath not seen thee oft amid thy store?
  Sometimes whoever seeks abroad may find
Thee sitting careless on a granary floor,
  Thy hair soft-lifted by the winnowing wind;
Or on a half-reap'd furrow sound asleep,
  Drows'd with the fume of poppies, while thy hook
    Spares the next swath and all its twined flowers:
And sometimes like a gleaner thou dost keep
  Steady thy laden head across a brook;
  Or by a cyder-press, with patient look,
    Thou watchest the last oozings hours by hours.

III

Where are the songs of Spring? Ay, where are they?
  Think not of them, thou hast thy music too,—

While barred clouds bloom the soft-dying day,
And touch the stubble-plains with rosy hue;
Then in a wailful choir the small gnats mourn
Among the river sallows, borne aloft
Or sinking as the light wind lives or dies;
And full-grown lambs loud bleat from hilly bourn;
Hedge-crickets sing; and now with treble soft
The red-breast whistles from a garden-croft;
And gathering swallows twitter in the skies.

V. Magic Casements

I have an idea that a Man might pass a very pleasant life in this manner—let him on any certain day read a certain Page of full Poesy or distilled Prose and let him wander with it, and muse upon it, and reflect from it, and bring home to it, and prophesy upon it, and dream upon it—until it becomes stale—but when will it do so? Never— When Man has arrived at a certain ripeness in intellect any one grand and spiritual passage serves him as a starting post towards all "the two-and thirty Pallaces." How happy is such a "voyage of conception," what delicious diligent Indolence!

—To J. H. Reynolds, February 19, 1818.

KEATS'S AXIOMS

In Poetry I have a few Axioms, and you will see how far I am from their Centre. 1st I think Poetry should surprise by a fine excess and not by Singularity—it should strike the Reader as a working of his own highest thoughts, and appear almost a Remembrance— 2nd Its touches of Beauty should never be half way thereby making the reader breathless instead of content: the rise, the progress, the setting of imagery should like the Sun come natural to him—shine over him and set soberly although in magnificence leaving him in the Luxury of twilight—but it is easier to think what Poetry should be than to write it—and this leads me on to another axiom. That if Poetry comes not as naturally as the Leaves to a tree it had better not come at all. However it may be with me I cannot help looking into new countries with 'O for a Muse of fire to ascend!'

—To John Taylor, February 27, 1818.

*As Tradesmen say every thing is worth what it will fetch, so prob-
ably every mental pursuit takes its reality and worth from the ardour of
the pursuer—being in itself a nothing—Ethereal thing[s] may at least
be thus real, divided under three heads—Things real—things semireal
—and no things—Things real—such as existences of Sun Moon &
Stars and passages of Shakspeare—Things semireal such as Love,
the Clouds &c which require a greeting of the Spirit to make them
wholly exist—and Nothings which are made Great and dignified by
an ardent pursuit.*

—To Benjamin Bailey, March 13, 1818.

LA BELLE DAME SANS MERCI

(First Version)

O WHAT can ail thee, Knight at arms,
   Alone and palely loitering?
The sedge has withered from the Lake
   And no birds sing!

O what can ail thee, Knight at arms,
   So haggard, and so woe begone?
The Squirrel's granary is full
   And the harvest's done.

I see a lily on thy brow
   With anguish moist and fever dew,
And on thy cheeks a fading rose
   Fast withereth too—

I met a Lady in the Meads,
   Full beautiful, a faery's child
Her hair was long, her foot was light
   And her eyes were wild—

I made a Garland for her head,
   And bracelets too, and fragrant Zone
She look'd at me as she did love
   And made sweet moan—

I set her on my pacing steed
   And nothing else saw all day long

For sidelong would she bend and sing
    A faery's song—

She found me roots of relish sweet
    And honey wild and manna dew
And sure in language strange she said
    I love thee true—

She took me to her elfin grot
    And there she wept and sigh'd full sore,
And there I shut her wild wild eyes
    With kisses four.

And there she lulled me asleep
    And there I dream'd, Ah Woe betide!
The latest dream I ever dreamt
    On the cold hill side.

I saw pale Kings, and Princes too
    Pale warriors, death pale were they all;
They cried, La belle dame sans merci
    Thee hath in thrall.

I saw their starv'd lips in the gloam
    With horrid warning gaped wide,
And I awoke, and found me here
    On the cold hill's side.

And this is why I sojourn here
    Alone and palely loitering;
Though the sedge is withered from the Lake
    And no birds sing——

THE EVE OF ST. AGNES

I

St. Agnes' Eve—Ah, bitter chill it was!
The owl, for all his feathers, was a-cold;
The hare limp'd trembling through the frozen grass,
And silent was the flock in woolly fold:
Numb were the Beadsman's fingers, while he told
His rosary, and while his frosted breath,
Like pious incense from a censer old,
Seem'd taking flight for heaven, without a death,
Past the sweet Virgin's picture, while his prayer he saith.

II

His prayer he saith, this patient, holy man;
Then takes his lamp, and riseth from his knees,
And back returneth, meagre, barefoot, wan,
Along the chapel aisle by slow degrees:
The sculptur'd dead, on each side, seem to freeze,
Emprison'd in black, purgatorial rails:
Knights, ladies, praying in dumb orat'ries,
He passeth by; and his weak spirit fails
To think how they may ache in icy hoods and mails.

III

Northward he turneth through a little door,
And scarce three steps, ere Music's golden tongue
Flatter'd to tears this aged man and poor;
But no—already had his deathbell rung:
The joys of all his life were said and sung:

His was harsh penance on St. Agnes' Eve:
Another way he went, and soon among
Rough ashes sat he for his soul's reprieve,
And all night kept awake, for sinners' sake to grieve.

IV

That ancient Beadsman heard the prelude soft;
And so it chanc'd, for many a door was wide,
From hurry to and fro. Soon, up aloft,
The silver, snarling trumpets 'gan to chide:
The level chambers, ready with their pride,
Were glowing to receive a thousand guests:
The carved angels, ever eager-eyed,
Star'd where upon their heads the cornice rests,
With hair blown back, and wings put cross-wise on
    their breasts.

V

At length burst in the argent revelry,
With plume, tiara, and all rich array,
Numerous as shadows haunting faerily
The brain, new stuff'd, in youth, with triumphs gay
Of old romance. These let us wish away,
And turn, sole-thoughted, to one Lady there,
Whose heart had brooded, all that wintry day,
On love, and wing'd St. Agnes' saintly care
As she had heard old dames full many times declare.

VI

They told her how, upon St. Agnes' Eve,
Young virgins might have visions of delight,
And soft adorings from their loves receive
Upon the honey'd middle of the night,

If ceremonies due they did aright;
As, supperless to bed they must retire,
And couch supine their beauties, lilly white;
Nor look behind, nor sideways, but require
Of Heaven with upward eyes for all that they desire.

VII

Full of this whim was thoughtful Madeline:
The music, yearning like a God in pain,
She scarcely heard: her maiden eyes divine,
Fix'd on the floor, saw many a sweeping train
Pass by—she heeded not at all: in vain
Came many a tiptoe, amorous cavalier,
And back retir'd; not cool'd by high disdain,
But she saw not: her heart was otherwhere:
She sigh'd for Agnes' dreams, the sweetest of the year.

VIII

She danc'd along with vague, regardless eyes,
Anxious her lips, her breathing quick and short:
The hallow'd hour was near at hand: she sighs
Amid the timbrels, and the throng'd resort
Of whisperers in anger, or in sport;
'Mid looks of love, defiance, hate, and scorn,
Hoodwink'd with faerily fancy; all amort,
Save to St. Agnes and her lambs unshorn,
And all the bliss to be before to-morrow morn.

IX

So, purposing each moment to retire,
She linger'd still. Meantime, across the moors,
Had come young Porphyro, with heart on fire
For Madeline. Beside the portal doors,

Buttress'd from moonlight, stands he, and implores
All saints to give him sight of Madeline,
But for one moment in the tedious hours,
That he might gaze and worship all unseen;
Perchance speak, kneel, touch, kiss—in sooth such
      things have been.

X

He ventures in: let no buzz'd whisper tell:
All eyes be muffled, or a hundred swords
Will storm his heart, Love's fev'rous citadel:
For him, those chambers held barbarian hordes,
Hyena foemen, and hot-blooded lords,
Whose very dogs would execrations howl
Against his lineage: not one breast affords
Him any mercy, in that mansion foul,
Save one old beldame, weak in body and in soul.

XI

Ah, happy chance! the aged creature came,
Shuffling along with ivory-headed wand,
To where he stood, hid from the torch's flame,
Behind a broad hall-pillar, far beyond
The sound of merriment and chorus bland:
He startled her; but soon she knew his face,
And grasp'd his fingers in her palsied hand,
Saying, "Mercy, Porphyro! hie thee from this place;
They are all here to-night, the whole blood-thirsty race!

XII

Get hence! get hence! there's dwarfish Hildebrand;
He had a fever late, and in the fit
He cursed thee and thine, both house and land:

72

Then there's that old Lord Maurice, not a whit
More tame for his gray hairs—Alas me! flit!
Flit like a ghost away,"—"Ah, Gossip dear,
We're safe enough; here in this arm-chair sit,
And tell me how"—"Good Saints! not here, not here;
Follow me, child, or else these stones will be thy bier."

XIII

He follow'd through a lowly arched way,
Brushing the cobwebs with his lofty plume,
And as she mutter'd "Well-a—well-a-day!"
He found him in a little moonlight room,
Pale, lattic'd, chill, and silent as a tomb.
"Now tell me where is Madeline," said he,
"O tell me, Angela, by the holy loom
Which none but secret sisterhood may see,
When they St. Agnes' wool are weaving piously."

XIV

"St. Agnes! Ah! it is St. Agnes' Eve—
Yet men will murder upon holy days:
Thou must hold water in a witch's sieve,
And be liege-lord of all the Elves and Fays,
To venture so: it fills me with amaze
To see thee, Porphyro!—St. Agnes' Eve!
God's help! my lady fair the conjuror plays
This very night: good angels her deceive!
But let me laugh awhile, I've mickle time to grieve."

XV

Feebly she laugheth in the languid moon,
While Porphyro upon her face doth look,
Like puzzled urchin on an aged crone

73

Who keepeth clos'd a wond'rous riddle-book,
As spectacled she sits in chimney nook.
But soon his eyes grew brilliant, when she told
His lady's purpose; and he scarce could brook
Tears, at the thought of those enchantments cold,
And Madeline asleep in lap of legends old.

XVI

Sudden a thought came like a full-blown rose,
Flushing his brow, and in his pained heart
Made purple riot: then doth he propose
A stratagem, that makes the beldame start:
"A cruel man and impious thou art:
Sweet lady, let her pray, and sleep, and dream
Alone with her good angels, far apart
From wicked men like thee. Go, go!—I deem
Thou canst not surely be the same that thou didst seem."

XVII

"I will not harm her, by all saints I swear,"
Quoth Porphyro: "O may I ne'er find grace
When my weak voice shall whisper its last prayer,
If one of her soft ringlets I displace,
Or look with ruffian passion in her face:
Good Angela, believe me by these tears;
Or I will, even in a moment's space,
Awake, with horrid shout, my foemen's ears,
And beard them, though they be more fang'd than
        wolves and bears."

XVIII

"Ah! why wilt thou affright a feeble soul?
A poor, weak, palsy-stricken, churchyard thing,

74

Whose passing-bell may ere the midnight toll;
Whose prayers for thee, each morn and evening,
Were never miss'd."—Thus plaining, doth she bring
A gentler speech from burning Porphyro;
So woful, and of such deep sorrowing,
That Angela gives promise she will do
Whatever he shall wish, betide her weal or woe.

XIX

Which was, to lead him, in close secrecy,
Even to Madeline's chamber, and there hide
Him in a closet, of such privacy
That he might see her beauty unespied,
And win perhaps that night a peerless bride,
While legion'd faeries pac'd the coverlet,
And pale enchantment held her sleepy-eyed.
Never on such a night have lovers met,
Since Merlin paid his Demon all the monstrous debt.

XX

"It shall be as thou wishest," said the Dame:
"All cates and dainties shall be stored there
Quickly on this feast-night: by the tambour frame
Her own lute thou wilt see: no time to spare,
For I am slow and feeble, and scarce dare
On such a catering trust my dizzy head.
Wait here, my child, with patience; kneel in prayer
The while: Ah! thou must needs the lady wed,
Or may I never leave my grave among the dead."

XXI

So saying, she hobbled off with busy fear.
The lover's endless minutes slowly pass'd:

The dame return'd, and whisper'd in his ear
To follow her; with aged eyes aghast
From fright of dim espial. Safe at last,
Through many a dusky gallery, they gain
The maiden's chamber, silken, hush'd, and chaste;
Where Porphyro took covert, pleas'd amain.
His poor guide hurried back with agues in her brain.

XXII

Her falt'ring hand upon the balustrade,
Old Angela was feeling for the stair,
When Madeline, St. Agnes' charmed maid,
Rose, like a mission'd spirit, unaware:
With silver taper's light, and pious care,
She turn'd, and down the aged gossip led
To a safe level matting. Now prepare,
Young Porphyro, for gazing on that bed;
She comes, she comes again, like ring-dove fray'd and
fled.

XXIII

Out went the taper as she hurried in;
Its little smoke, in pallid moonshine, died:
She clos'd the door, she panted, all akin
To spirits of the air, and visions wide:
No uttered syllable, or, woe betide!
But to her heart, her heart was voluble,
Paining with eloquence her balmy side;
As though a tongueless nightingale should swell
Her heart in vain, and die, heart-stifled, in her dell.

76

XXIV

A casement high and triple-arch'd there was,
All garlanded with carven imag'ries
Of fruits, and flowers, and bunches of knot-grass,
And diamonded with panes of quaint device,
Innumerable of stains and splendid dyes,
As are the tiger-moth's deep-damask'd wings;
And in the midst, 'mong thousand heraldries,
And twilight saints, and dim emblazonings,
A shielded scutcheon blush'd with blood of queens and
    kings.

XXV

Full on this casement shone the wintry moon,
And threw warm gules on Madeline's fair breast,
As down she knelt for heaven's grace and boon;
Rose-bloom fell on her hands, together prest,
And on her silver cross soft amethyst,
And on her hair a glory, like a saint:
She seem'd a splendid angel, newly drest,
Save wings, for heaven:—Porphyro grew faint:
She knelt, so pure a thing, so free from mortal taint.

XXVI

Anon his heart revives: her vespers done,
Of all its wreathed pearls her hair she frees;
Unclasps her warmed jewels one by one;
Loosens her fragrant boddice; by degrees
Her rich attire creeps rustling to her knees:
Half-hidden, like a mermaid in sea-weed,
Pensive awhile she dreams awake, and sees,
In fancy, fair St. Agnes in her bed,
But dares not look behind, or all the charm is fled.

XXVII

Soon trembling in her soft and chilly nest,
In sort of wakeful swoon, perplex'd she lay,
Until the poppied warmth of sleep oppress'd
Her soothed limbs, and soul fatigued away;
Flown, like a thought, until the morrow-day;
Blissfully haven'd both from joy and pain;
Clasp'd like a missal where swart Paynims pray;
Blinded alike from sunshine and from rain,
As though a rose should shut, and be a bud again.

XXVIII

Stol'n to this paradise, and so entranced,
Porphyro gazed upon her empty dress,
And listen'd to her breathing, if it chanced
To wake into a slumberous tenderness;
Which when he heard, that minute did he bless,
And breath'd himself: then from the closet crept,
Noiseless as fear in a wide wilderness,
And over the hush'd carpet, silent, stept,
And 'tween the curtains peep'd, where, lo!—how fast
    she slept.

Then by the bed-side, where the faded moon
Made a dim, silver twilight, soft he set
A table, and, half anguish'd, threw thereon
A cloth of woven crimson, gold, and jet:—
O for some drowsy Morphean amulet!
The boisterous, midnight, festive clarion,
The kettle-drum, and far-heard clarinet,
Affray his ears, though but in dying tone:—
The hall door shuts again, and all the noise is gone.

And still she slept an azure-lidded sleep,
In blanched linen, smooth, and lavender'd,
While he from forth the closet brought a heap
Of candied apple, quince, and plum, and gourd;
With jellies soother than the creamy curd,
And lucent syrops, tinct with cinnamon;
Manna and dates, in argosy transferr'd
From Fez; and spiced dainties, every one,
From silken Samarcand to cedar'd Lebanon.

XXXI

These delicates he heap'd with glowing hand
On golden dishes and in baskets bright
Of wreathed silver: sumptuous they stand
In the retired quiet of the night,
Filling the chilly room with perfume light.—
"And now, my love, my seraph fair, awake!
Thou art my heaven, and I thine eremite:
Open thine eyes, for meek St. Agnes' sake,
Or I shall drowse beside thee, so my soul doth ache."

Thus whispering, his warm, unnerved arm
Sank in her pillow. Shaded was her dream
By the dusk curtains:—'twas a midnight charm
Impossible to melt as iced stream:
The lustrous salvers in the moonlight gleam;
Broad golden fringe upon the carpet lies:
It seem'd he never, never could redeem
From such a stedfast spell his lady's eyes;
So mus'd awhile, entoil'd in woofed phantasies.

Awakening up, he took her hollow lute,—
Tumultuous,—and, in chords that tenderest be,
He play'd an ancient ditty, long since mute,
In Provence call'd, "La belle dame sans mercy:"
Close to her ear touching the melody;—
Wherewith disturb'd, she utter'd a soft moan:
He ceased—she panted quick—and suddenly
Her blue affrayed eyes wide open shone:
Upon his knees he sank, pale as smooth sculptured stone.

XXXIV

Her eyes were open, but she still beheld,
Now wide awake, the vision of her sleep:
There was a painful change, that nigh expell'd
The blisses of her dream so pure and deep
At which fair Madeline began to weep,
And moan forth witless words with many a sigh;
While still her gaze on Porphyro would keep;
Who knelt, with joined hands and piteous eye,
Fearing to move or speak, she look'd so dreamingly.

"Ah, Porphyro!" said she, "but even now
Thy voice was at sweet tremble in mine ear,
Made tuneable with every sweetest vow;
And those sad eyes were spiritual and clear:
How chang'd thou art! how pallid, chill, and drear!
Give me that voice again, my Porphyro,
Those looks immortal, those complainings dear!
Oh leave me not in this eternal woe,
For if thou diest, my Love, I know not where to go."

Beyond a mortal man impassion'd far
At these voluptuous accents, he arose,
Ethereal, flush'd, and like a throbbing star
Seen mid the sapphire heaven's deep repose;
Into her dream he melted, as the rose
Blendeth its odour with the violet,—
Solution sweet: meantime the frost-wind blows
Like Love's alarum pattering the sharp sleet
Against the window-panes; St. Agnes' moon hath set.

XXXVII

'Tis dark: quick pattereth the flaw-blown sleet:
"This is no dream, my bride, my Madeline!"
'Tis dark: the iced gusts still rave and beat:
"No dream, alas! alas! and woe is mine!
Porphyro will leave me here to fade and pine.—
Cruel! what traitor could thee hither bring?
I curse not, for my heart is lost in thine,
Though thou forsakest a deceived thing;—
A dove forlorn and lost with sick unpruned wing."

"My Madeline! sweet dreamer! lovely bride!
Say, may I be for aye thy vassal blest?
Thy beauty's shield, heart-shap'd and vermeil dyed?
Ah, silver shrine, here will I take my rest
After so many hours of toil and quest,
A famish'd pilgrim,—sav'd by miracle.
Though I have found, I will not rob thy nest
Saving of thy sweet self; if thou think'st well
To trust, fair Madeline, to no rude infidel.

"Hark! 'tis an elfin-storm from faery land,
  Of haggard seeming, but a boon indeed:
Arise—arise! the morning is at hand;—
  The bloated wassaillers will never heed:—
  Let us away, my love, with happy speed;
There are no ears to hear, or eyes to see,—
  Drown'd all in Rhenish and the sleepy mead:
Awake! arise! my love, and fearless be,
For o'er the southern moors I have a home for thee."

XL

She hurried at his words, beset with fears,
  For there were sleeping dragons all around,
At glaring watch, perhaps, with ready spears—
  Down the wide stairs a darkling way they found.—
  In all the house was heard no human sound.
A chain-droop'd lamp was flickering by each door;
  The arras, rich with horseman, hawk, and hound,
Flutter'd in the besieging wind's uproar;
And the long carpets rose along the gusty floor.

They glide, like phantoms, into the wide hall!
  Like phantoms, to the iron porch, they glide;
Where lay the Porter, in uneasy sprawl,
  With a huge empty flaggon by his side:
  The wakeful bloodhound rose, and shook his hide,
But his sagacious eye an inmate owns:
  By one, and one, the bolts full easy slide:—
The chains lie silent on the footworn stones;—
The key turns, and the door upon its hinges groans.

And they are gone: aye, ages long ago
These lovers fled away into the storm.
That night the Baron dreamt of many a woe,
And all his warrior-guests, with shade and form
Of witch, and demon, and large coffin-worm,
Were long be-nightmar'd. Angela the old
Died palsy-twitch'd, with meagre face deform;
The Beadsman, after thousand aves told,
For aye unsought for slept among his ashes cold.

VI. Light and Incidental Verse

"HOW BEAUTIFUL ARE THE RETIRED FLOWERS!"

We hate poetry that has a palpable design upon us—and if we do not agree, seems to put its hand in its breeches pocket. Poetry should be great & unobtrusive, a thing which enters into one's soul, and does not startle it or amaze it with itself but with its subject.—How beautiful are the retired flowers! how would they lose their beauty were they to throng into the highway crying out, "admire me I am a violet! dote upon me I am a primrose!"

—To J. H. Reynolds, February 3, 1818.

LANDSCAPE AND HUMAN NATURE

Scenery is fine—but human nature is finer—The Sward is richer for the tread of a real, nervous, english foot—the eagles nest is finer for the Mountaineer has look'd into it.

—To Benjamin Bailey, March 13, 1818.

I HAD A DOVE

I HAD A DOVE and the sweet dove died,
And I have thought it died of grieving:
O, what could it grieve for? Its feet were tied
With a silken thread of my own hand's weaving;
Sweet little red feet! why should you die—
Why should you leave me, sweet bird! why?
You liv'd alone in the forest-tree,
Why, pretty thing! would you not live with me?
I kiss'd you oft and gave you white peas;
Why not live sweetly, as in the green trees?

I

In a drear-nighted December,
Too happy, happy tree,
Thy branches ne'er remember
Their green felicity:
The north cannot undo them
With a sleety whistle through them;
From budding at the prime.

II

In a drear-nighted December,
Too happy, happy brook,
Thy bubblings ne'er remember
Apollo's summer look;
But with a sweet forgetting,
They stay their crystal fretting,
Never, never petting
About the frozen time.

III

Ah! would 'twere so with many
A gentle girl and boy!
But were there ever any
Writh'd not at passed joy?
"The feel of *not* to feel it,"
When there is none to heal it
Nor numbed sense to steel it,
Was never said in rhyme.

ROBIN HOOD

No! those days are gone away,
And their hours are old and gray,
And their minutes buried all
Under the down-trodden pall
Of the leaves of many years:
Many times have winter's shears,
Frozen North, and chilling East,
Sounded tempests to the feast
Of the forest's whispering fleeces,
Since men knew nor rent nor leases.

No, the bugle sounds no more,
And the twanging bow no more;
Silent is the ivory shrill
Past the heath and up the hill;
There is no mid-forest laugh,
Where lone Echo gives the half
To some wight, amaz'd to hear
Jesting, deep in forest drear.

On the fairest time of June
You may go, with sun or moon,
Or the seven stars to light you,
Or the polar ray to right you;
But you never may behold
Little John, or Robin bold;
Never one, of all the clan,
Thrumming on an empty can

Some old hunting ditty, while
He doth his green way beguile
To fair hostess Merriment,
Down beside the pasture Trent;
For he left the merry tale
Messenger for spicy ale.

Gone, the merry morris din;
Gone, the song of Gamelyn;
Gone, the tough-belted outlaw
Idling in the "'grenè shawe";
All are gone away and past!
And if Robin should be cast
Sudden from his turfed grave,
And if Marian should have
Once again her forest days,
She would weep, and he would craze:
He would swear, for all his oaks,
Fall'n beneath the dockyard strokes,
Have rotted on the briny seas;
She would weep that her wild bees
Sang not to her—strange! that honey
Can't be got without hard money!

So it is: yet let us sing,
Honour to the old bow-string!
Honour to the bugle-horn!
Honour to the woods unshorn!
Honour to the Lincoln green!
Honour to the archer keen!
Honour to tight little John,
And the horse he rode upon!
Honour to bold Robin Hood,

Sleeping in the underwood!
Honour to maid Marian,
And to all the Sherwood-clan!
Though their days have hurried by
Let us two a burden try.

OH, I AM FRIGHTEN'D WITH MOST HATEFUL THOUGHTS

OH, I am frighten'd with most hateful thoughts!
Perhaps her voice is not a nightingale's,
Perhaps her teeth are not the fairest pearl;
Her eye-lashes may be, for aught I know,
Not longer than the May-fly's small fan-horns;
There may not be one dimple on her hand;
And freckles many; ah! a careless nurse,
In haste to teach the little thing to walk,
May have crumpt up a pair of Dian's legs,
And warpt the ivory of a Juno's neck.

DEAR REYNOLDS! I have a mysterious tale,
And cannot speak it: the first page I read
Upon a Lampit rock of green sea-weed
Among the breakers; 'twas a quiet eve,
The rocks were silent, the wide sea did weave
An untumultuous fringe of silver foam
Along the flat brown sand; I was at home
And should have been most happy,—but I saw
Too far into the sea, where every maw
The greater on the less feeds evermore.—
But I saw too distinct into the core
Of an eternal fierce destruction,
And so from happiness I far was gone.
Still am I sick of it, and tho', to-day,
I've gather'd young spring-leaves, and flowers gay
Of periwinkle and wild strawberry,
Still do I that most fierce destruction see,—
The Shark at savage prey,—the Hawk at pounce,—
The gentle Robin, like a Pard or Ounce,
Ravening a worm,—Away, ye horrid moods!
Moods of one's mind! You know I hate them well.
You know I'd sooner be a clapping Bell
To some Kamtschatcan Missionary Church,
Than with these horrid moods be left i' the lurch.

SOULS OF POETS dead and gone,
What Elysium have ye known,
Happy field or mossy cavern,
Choicer than the Mermaid Tavern?
Have ye tippled drink more fine
Than mine host's Canary wine?
Or are fruits of Paradise
Sweeter than those dainty pies
Of venison? O generous food!
Drest as though bold Robin Hood
Would, with his maid Marian,
Sup and bowse from horn and can.

I have heard that on a day
Mine host's sign-board flew away,
Nobody knew whither, till
An astrologer's old quill
To a sheepskin gave the story,
Said he saw you in your glory,
Underneath a new old sign
Sipping beverage divine,
And pledging with contented smack
The Mermaid in the Zodiac.

Souls of Poets dead and gone,
What Elysium have ye known,
Happy field or mossy cavern,
Choicer than the Mermaid Tavern?

DAISY'S SONG

I

THE SUN, with his great eye,
Sees not so much as I;
And the moon, all silver-proud,
Might as well be in a cloud.

II

And O the spring—the spring
I lead the life of a king!
Couch'd in the teeming grass,
I spy each pretty lass.

III

I look where no one dares,
And I stare where no one stares,
And when the night is nigh,
Lambs bleat my lullaby.

FOLLY'S SONG

WHEN wedding fiddles are a-playing,
    Huzza for folly O!
And when maidens go a-Maying,
    Huzza, &c.
When a milk-pail is upset,
    Huzza, &c.
And the clothes left in the wet,
    Huzza, &c.
When the barrel's set abroach,
    Huzza, &c.
When Kate Eyebrow keeps a coach,
    Huzza, &c.
When the pig is over-roasted,
    Huzza, &c.
And the cheese is over-toasted,
    Huzza, &c.
When Sir Snap is with his lawyer,
    Huzza, &c.
And Miss Chip has kiss'd the sawyer,
    Huzza, &c.

THE DEVON MAID

Stanzas Sent in a Letter to B. R. Haydon

I

WHERE be ye going, you Devon Maid?
   And what have ye there in the basket?
Ye tight little fairy just fresh from the dairy,
   Will ye give me some cream if I ask it?

II

I love your Meads, and I love your flowers,
   And I love your junkets mainly,
But 'hind the door I love kissing more,
   O look not so disdainly.

III

I love your hills, and I love your dales,
   And I love your flocks a-bleating—
But O, on the heather to lie together,
   With both our hearts a-beating!

IV

I'll put your basket all safe in a nook;
   Your shawl I'll hang up on the willow;
And we will sigh in the daisy's eye
   And kiss on a grass green pillow.

DAWLISH FAIR

OVER THE HILL and over the Dale,
  And over the Bourne to Dawlish,
Where ginger-bread wives have a scanty sale,
  And ginger-bread nuts are smallish

Rantipole Betty she ran down a hill
  And kick'd up her petticoats fairly:
Says I I'll be Jack if you will be Gill.
  So she lay on the grass debonnairly.

"Here's somebody coming, here's somebody coming!"
  Says I 'tis the wind at a parley;
So without any fuss any hawing or humming
  She lay on the grass debonnairly.—

"Here's somebody here, and here's somebody there,"
  Says I hold your tongue you young Gipsey.
So she held her tongue and lay plump and fair,
  As dead as a Venus tipsy.

O who wouldn't hie to Dawlish fair,
  O who wouldn't stop in a Meadow,
O [who] wouldn't rumple the daisies there,
  And make the wild fern for a bed do?

I

THERE WAS a naughty Boy,
    And a naughty boy was he,
He would not stop at home,
    He could not quiet be—
        He took
        In his Knapsack
        A Book
        Full of vowels
        And a shirt
        With some towels—
        A slight cap
        For night cap—
        A hair brush,
        Comb ditto,
        New Stockings
        For old ones
        Would split O!
        This Knapsack
        Tight at's back
        He rivetted close
And follow'd his nose
        To the North,
        To the North,
And follow'd his nose
        To the North.

There was a naughty boy
  And a naughty boy was he,
For nothing would he do
  But scribble poetry—
        He took
        An ink stand
        In his hand
        And a pen
        Big as ten
        In the other,
        And away
        In a Pother
        He ran
        To the mountains
        And fountains
        And ghostes
        And Postes
        And witches
        And ditches
        And wrote
        In his coat
        When the weather
        Was cool,
        Fear of gout,
        And without
        When the weather
        Was warm—
        Och the charm
        When we choose
    To follow one's nose
        To the north,
        To the north,

To follow one's nose
To the north!

III

There was a naughty boy
And a naughty boy was he,
He kept little fishes
In washing tubs three
In spite
Of the might
Of the Maid
Nor afraid
Of his Granny-good—
He often would
Hurly burly
Get up early
And go
By hook or crook
To the brook
And bring home
Miller's thumb,
Tittlebat
Not over fat,
Minnows small
As the stall
Of a glove,
Not above
The size
Of a nice
Little Baby's
Little fingers—
O he made
'Twas his trade

Of Fish a Pretty Kettle
    A Kettle—
    A Kettle
Of Fish a pretty Kettle
    A Kettle!

There was a naughty Boy,
    And a naughty Boy was he,
He ran away to Scotland
    The people for to see—
        Then he found
        That the ground
        Was as hard,
        That a yard
        Was as long,
        That a song
        Was as merry,
        That a cherry
        Was as red—
        That lead
        Was as weighty,
        That fourscore
        Was as eighty,
        That a door
        Was as wooden
        As in England—
So he stood in his shoes
    And he wonder'd,
    He wonder'd,
He stood in his shoes
    And he wonder'd.

OLD MEG she was a Gipsy,
    And liv'd upon the Moors:
Her bed it was the brown heath turf,
    And her house was out-of-doors.

Her apples were swart blackberries,
    Her currants pods o' broom;
Her wine was dew of the wild white rose,
    Her book a churchyard tomb.

Her Brothers were the craggy hills,
    Her Sisters larchen trees—
Alone with her great family
    She liv'd as she did please.

No breakfast had she many a morn,
    No dinner many a noon,
And 'stead of supper she would stare
    Full hard against the Moon.

But every morn of woodbine fresh
    She made her garlanding,
And every night the dark glen Yew
    She wove, and she would sing.

And with her fingers old and brown
    She plaited Mats o' Rushes,

And gave them to the Cottagers
    She met among the Bushes.

Old Meg was brave as Margaret Queen
    And tall as Amazon:
An old red blanket cloak she wore;
A chip hat had she on.
God rest her aged bones somewhere—
    She died full long agone!

FANCY

Ever let the fancy roam,
Pleasure never is at home:
At a touch sweet Pleasure melteth,
Like to bubbles when rain pelteth;
Then let winged Fancy wander
Through the thought still spread beyond her:
Open wide the mind's cage-door,
She'll dart forth, and cloudward soar.
O sweet Fancy! let her loose;
Summer's joys are spoilt by use,
And the enjoying of the Spring
Fades as does its blossoming;
Autumn's red-lipp'd fruitage too,
Blushing through the mist and dew,
Cloys with tasting: What do then?
Sit thee by the ingle, when
The sear faggot blazes bright,
Spirit of a winter's night;
When the soundless earth is muffled,
And the caked snow is shuffled
From the ploughboy's heavy shoon;
When the Night doth meet the Noon
In a dark conspiracy
To banish Even from her sky.
Sit thee there, and send abroad,
With a mind self-overaw'd,
Fancy, high-commission'd:—send her!
She has vassals to attend her:
She will bring, in spite of frost,

Beauties that the earth hath lost;
She will bring thee, all together,
All delights of summer weather;
All the buds and bells of May,
From dewy sward or thorny spray;
All the heaped Autumn's wealth,
With a still, mysterious stealth:
She will mix these pleasures up
Like three fit wines in a cup,
And thou shalt quaff it:—thou shalt hear
Distant harvest-carols clear;
Rustle of the reaped corn;
Sweet birds antheming the morn:
And, in the same moment—hark!
'Tis the early April lark,
Or the rooks, with busy caw,
Foraging for sticks and straw.
Thou shalt, at one glance, behold
The daisy and the marigold;
White-plum'd lillies, and the first
Hedge-grown primrose that hath burst;
Shaded hyacinth, alway
Sapphire queen of the mid-May;
And every leaf, and every flower
Pearled with the self-same shower.
Thou shalt see the field-mouse peep
Meagre from its celled sleep;
And the snake all winter-thin
Cast on sunny bank its skin;
Freckled nest-eggs thou shalt see
Hatching in the hawthorn-tree,
When the hen-bird's wing doth rest
Quiet on her mossy nest;

Then the hurry and alarm
When the bee-hive casts its swarm;
Acorns ripe down-pattering,
While the autumn breezes sing.

Oh, sweet Fancy! let her loose;
Every thing is spoilt by use:
Where's the cheek that doth not fade,
Too much gaz'd at? Where's the maid
Whose lip mature is ever new?
Where's the eye, however blue,
Doth not weary? Where's the face
One would meet in every place?
Where's the voice, however soft,
One would hear so very oft?
At a touch sweet Pleasure melteth
Like the bubbles when rain pelteth.
Let, then, winged Fancy find
Thee a mistress to thy mind:
Dulcet-eyed as Ceres' daughter,
Ere the God of Torment taught her
How to frown and how to chide;
With a waist and with a side
White as Hebe's, when her zone
Slipt its golden clasp, and down
Fell her kirtle to her feet,
While she held the goblet sweet,
And Jove grew languid.—Break the mesh
Of the Fancy's silken leash;
Quickly break her prison-string
And such joys as these she'll bring.—
Let the winged Fancy roam,
Pleasure never is at home.

TWO OR THREE

From a Letter to His Sister

Two or three Posies
With two or three simples—
Two or three Noses
With two or three pimples—
Two or three wise men
And two or three ninnies—
Two or three purses
And two or three guineas—
Two or three raps
At two or three doors—
Two or three naps
Of two or three hours—
Two or three Cats
And two or three mice—
Two or three sprats
At a very great price—
Two or three sandies
And two or three tabbies—
Two or three dandies
And two Mrs.—— mum!
Two or three Smiles
And two or three frowns—
Two or three Miles
To two or three towns—
Two or three pegs
For two or three bonnets—
Two or three dove eggs
To hatch into sonnets.

VII. The Two Hyperions

"PROVED UPON OUR PULSES"

Axioms in philosophy are not axioms until they are proved upon our pulses: We read fine things but never feel them to the full until we have gone the same steps as the Author.—I know this is not plain; you will know exactly my meaning when I say, that now I shall relish Hamlet more than I ever have done—Or, better—You are sensible no man can set down Venery as a bestial or joyless thing until he is sick of it and therefore all philosophizing on it would be mere wording. Until we are sick, we understand not;—in fine, as Byron says, "Knowledge is Sorrow"; and I go on to say that "Sorrow is Wisdom"—and further for aught we can know for certainty! "Wisdom is folly."

IN THE MANSION OF LIFE

I compare human life to a large Mansion of Many Apartments, two of which I can only describe, the doors of the rest being as yet shut upon me—The first we step into we call the infant or thoughtless Chamber, in which we remain as long as we do not think—We remain there a long while, and notwithstanding the doors of the second Chamber remain wide open, showing a bright appearance, we care not to hasten to it; but are at length imperceptibly impelled by the awakening of the thinking principle within us—we no sooner get into the second Chamber, which I shall call the Chamber of Maiden-Thought, than we become intoxicated with the light and the atmosphere, we see nothing but pleasant wonders, and think of delaying there for ever in delight: However among the effects this breathing is father of is that tremendous one of sharpening one's vision into the heart and nature of Man—of convincing one's nerves that the World is full of Misery and Heartbreak, Pain, Sickness and oppression—whereby This Chamber of Maiden Thought becomes gradually darken'd and at the same time on all sides of it many doors are set open—but all dark—all leading to dark passages

—We see not the ballance of good and evil. We are in a Mist—We are now in that state—We feel the "burden of the Mystery," To this point was Wordsworth come, as far as I can conceive when he wrote 'Tintern Abbey' and it seems to me that his Genius is explorative of those dark Passages. Now if we live, and go on thinking, we too shall explore them.

—To J. H. Reynolds, May 3, 1818.

"A LOAD OF IMMORTALITY"

This morning Poetry has conquered—I have relapsed into those abstractions [the writing of Hyperion] *which are my only life—I feel escaped from a new strange and threatening sorrow.—And I am thankful for it—There is an awful warmth about my heart like a load of Immortality.*

—To J. H. Reynolds, September, 1818.

"A LIFE OF ALLEGORY"

1

A Man's life of any worth is a continual allegory—and very few eyes can see the Mystery of his life—a life like the scriptures, figurative —which such people can no more make out than they can the hebrew Bible. Lord Byron cuts a figure—but he is not figurative—Shakspeare led a life of Allegory; his works are the comments on it. . . .

2

Nothing ever becomes real till it is experienced—Even a Proverb is no proverb to you till your Life has illustrated it.

—To George and Georgiana Keats, February-March, 1819.

DEEP in the shady sadness of a vale
Far sunken from the healthy breath of morn,
Far from the fiery noon, and eve's one star,
Sat gray-hair'd Saturn, quiet as a stone,
Still as the silence round about his lair;
Forest on forest hung about his head
Like cloud on cloud. No stir of air was there,
Not so much life as on a summer's day
Robs not one light seed from the feather'd grass,
But where the dead leaf fell, there did it rest.
A stream went voiceless by, still deadened more
By reason of his fallen divinity
Spreading a shade: the Naiad 'mid her reeds
Press'd her cold finger closer to her lips.

Along the margin-sand large foot-marks went,
No further than to where his feet had stray'd.
And slept there since. Upon the sodden ground
His old right hand lay nerveless, listless, dead,
Unsceptred; and his realmless eyes were closed;
While his bow'd head seem'd list'ning to the Earth,
His ancient mother, for some comfort yet.

It seem'd no force could wake him from his place;
But there came one, who with a kindred hand
Touch'd his wide shoulders, after bending low
With reverence, though to one who knew it not.
She was a Goddess of the infant world;
By her in stature the tall Amazon
Had stood a pigmy's height: she would have ta'en

Achilles by the hair and bent his neck;
Or with a finger stay'd Ixion's wheel.
Her face was large as that of Memphian sphinx,
Pedestal'd haply in a palace court,
When sages look'd to Egypt for their lore.
But oh! how unlike marble was that face:
How beautiful, if sorrow had not made
Sorrow more beautiful than Beauty's self.
There was a listening fear in her regard,
As if calamity had but begun;
As if the vanward clouds of evil days
Had spent their malice, and the sullen rear
Was with its stored thunder labouring up.
One hand she press'd upon that aching spot
Where beats the human heart, as if just there,
Though an immortal, she felt cruel pain:
The other upon Saturn's bended neck
She laid, and to the level of his ear
Leaning with parted lips, some words she spake
In solemn tenour and deep organ tone:
Some mourning words, which in our feeble tongue
Would come in these like accents; O how frail
To that large utterance of the early Gods!
"Saturn, look up!—though wherefore, poor old King?
I have no comfort for thee, no not one:
I cannot say, 'O wherefore sleepest thou?'
For heaven is parted from thee, and the earth
Knows thee not, thus afflicted, for a God;
And ocean too, with all its solemn noise,
Has from thy sceptre pass'd; and all the air
Is emptied of thine hoary majesty.
Thy thunder, conscious of the new command,
Rumbles reluctant o'er our fallen house;

And thy sharp lightning in unpractised hands
Scorches and burns our once serene domain.
O aching time! O moments big as years!
All as ye pass swell out the monstrous truth,
And press it so upon our weary griefs
That unbelief has not a space to breathe.
Saturn, sleep on:—O thoughtless, why did I
Thus violate thy slumbrous solitude?
Why should I ope thy melancholy eyes?
Saturn, sleep on! while at thy feet I weep."

  As when, upon a tranced summer-night,
Those green-rob'd senators of mighty woods,
Tall oaks, branch-charmed by the earnest stars,
Dream, and so dream all night without a stir,
Save from one gradual solitary gust
Which comes upon the silence, and dies off,
As if the ebbing air had but one wave;
So came these words and went; the while in tears
She touch'd her fair large forehead to the ground,
Just where her falling hair might be outspread
A soft and silken mat for Saturn's feet.
One moon, with alteration slow, had shed
Her silver seasons four upon the night,
And still these two were postured motionless,
Like natural sculpture in cathedral cavern;
The frozen God still couchant on the earth,
And the sad Goddess weeping at his feet:
Until at length old Saturn lifted up
His faded eyes, and saw his kingdom gone,
And all the gloom and sorrow of the place,
And that fair kneeling Goddess; and then spake,
As with a palsied tongue, and while his beard

Shook horrid with such aspen-malady:
"O tender spouse of gold Hyperion,
Thea, I feel thee ere I see thy face;
Look up, and let me see our doom in it;
Look up, and tell me if this feeble shape
Is Saturn's; tell me, if thou hear'st the voice
Of Saturn; tell me, if this wrinkling brow,
Naked and bare of its great diadem,
Peers like the front of Saturn. Who had power
To make me desolate? whence came the strength?
How was it nurtur'd to such bursting forth,
While Fate seem'd strangled in my nervous grasp?
But it is so; and I am smother'd up,
And buried from all godlike exercise
Of influence benign on planets pale,
Of admonitions to the winds and seas,
Of peaceful sway above man's harvesting,
And all those acts which Deity supreme
Doth ease its heart of love in.—I am gone
Away from my own bosom: I have left
My strong identity, my real self,
Somewhere between the throne, and where I sit
Here on this spot of earth. Search, Thea, search!
Open thine eyes eterne, and sphere them round
Upon all space: space starr'd, and lorn of light;
Space region'd with life-air; and barren void;
Spaces of fire, and all the yawn of hell.—
Search, Thea, search! and tell me, if thou seest
A certain shape or shadow, making way
With wings or chariot fierce to repossess
A heaven he lost erewhile: it must—it must
Be of ripe progress—Saturn must be King.
Yes, there must be a golden victory;

There must be Gods thrown down, and trumpets blown
Of triumph calm, and hymns of festival
Upon the gold clouds metropolitan,
Voices of soft proclaim, and silver stir
Of strings in hollow shells: and there shall be
Beautiful things made new, for the surprise
Of the sky-children; I will give command:
Thea! Thea! Thea! where is Saturn?"

This passion lifted him upon his feet,
And made his hands to struggle in the air,
His Druid locks to shake and ooze with sweat,
His eyes to fever out, his voice to cease.
He stood, and heard not Thea's sobbing deep;
A little time, and then again he snatch'd
Utterance thus.—"But cannot I create?
Cannot I form? Cannot I fashion forth
Another world, another universe,
To overbear and crumble this to naught?
Where is another chaos? Where?"—That word
Found way unto Olympus, and made quake
The rebel three.—Thea was startled up,
And in her bearing was a sort of hope,
As thus she quick-voic'd spake, yet full of awe.

"This cheers our fallen house: come to our friends,
O Saturn! come away, and give them heart;
I know the covert, for thence came I hither."
Thus brief; then with beseeching eyes she went
With backward footing through the shade a space:
He follow'd, and she turn'd to lead the way
Through aged boughs, that yielded like the mist
Which eagles cleave upmounting from their nest.

Meanwhile in other realms big tears were shed,
More sorrow like to this, and such like woe,
Too huge for mortal tongue or pen of scribe:
The Titans fierce,, self-hid or prison-bound,
Groan'd for the old allegiance once more,
And listen'd in sharp pain for Saturn's voice.
But one of the whole mammoth-brood still kept
His sov'reignty, and rule, and majesty;—
Blazing Hyperion on his orbed fire
Still sat, still snuff'd the incense, teeming up
From man to the sun's God; yet unsecure:
For as among us mortals omens drear
Fright and perplex, so also shuddered he—
Not as dog's howl, or gloom-bird's hated screech,
Or the familiar visiting of one
Upon the first toll of his passing-bell,
Or prophesyings of the midnight lamp;
But horrors, portion'd to a giant nerve,
Oft made Hyperion ache. His palace bright
Bastion'd with pyramids of glowing gold,
And touch'd with shade of bronzed obelisks,
Glar'd a blood-red through all its thousand courts,
Arches, and domes, and fiery galleries;
And all its curtains of Aurorian clouds
Flush'd angerly: while sometimes eagle's wings,
Unseen before by Gods or wondering men,
Darken'd the place; and neighing steeds were heard,
Not heard before by Gods or wondering men.
Also, when he would taste the spicy wreaths
Of incense, breath'd aloft from sacred hills,
Instead of sweets, his ample palate took
Savour of poisonous brass and metal sick:
And so, when harbour'd in the sleepy west,

After the full completion of fair day,—
For rest divine upon exalted couch
And slumber in the arms of melody,
He pac'd away the pleasant hours of ease
With stride colossal, on from hall to hall;
While far within each aisle and deep recess,
His winged minions in close clusters stood,
Amaz'd and full of fear; like anxious men
Who on wide plains gather in panting troops,
When earthquakes jar their battlements and towers.
Even now, while Saturn, rous'd from icy trance,
Went step for step with Thea through the woods,
Hyperion, leaving twilight in the rear,
Came slope upon the threshold of the west;
Then, as was wont, his palace-door flew ope
In smoothest silence, save what solemn tubes,
Blown by the serious Zephyrs, gave of sweet
And wandering sounds, slow-breathed melodies;
And like a rose in vermeil tint and shape,
In fragrance soft, and coolness to the eye,
That inlet to severe magnificence
Stood full blown, for the God to enter in.

   He enter'd, but he enter'd full of wrath;
His flaming robes stream'd out beyond his heels,
And gave a roar, as if of earthly fire,
That scar'd away the meek ethereal Hours
And made their dove-wings tremble. On he flared,
From stately nave to nave, from vault to vault,
Through bowers of fragrant and enwreathed light,
And diamond-paved lustrous long arcades,
Until he reach'd the great main cupola;
There standing fierce beneath, he stamped his foot,

And bid the day begin, if but for change.
He might not:—No, though a primeval God:
The sacred seasons might not be disturb'd.
Therefore the operations of the dawn
Stay'd in their birth, even as here 'tis told.
Those silver wings expanded sisterly,
Eager to sail their orb; the porches wide
Open'd upon the dusk demesnes of night;
And the bright Titan, phrenzied with new woes,
Unus'd to bend, by hard compulsion bent
His spirit to the sorrow of the time;
And all along a dismal rack of clouds,
Upon the boundaries of day and night,
He stretch'd himself in grief and radiance faint.
There as he lay, the Heaven with its stars
Look'd down on him with pity, and the voice
Of Cœlus, from the universal space,
Thus whisper'd low and solemn in his ear.
"O brightest of my children dear, earth-born
And sky-engendered, Son of Mysteries
All unrevealed even to the powers
Which met at thy creating; at whose joys
And palpitations sweet, and pleasures soft,
I, Cœlus, wonder, how they came and whence;
And at the fruits thereof what shapes they be,
Distinct, and visible; symbols divine,
Manifestations of that beauteous life
Diffus'd unseen throughout eternal space:
Of these new-form'd art thou, oh brightest child!
Of these, thy brethren and the Goddesses!
There is sad feud among ye, and rebellion
Of son against his sire. I saw him fall,
I saw my first-born tumbled from his throne!
To me his arms were spread, to me his voice

Found way from forth the thunders round his head!
Pale wox I, and in vapours hid my face.
Art thou, too, near such doom? vague fear there is:
For I have seen my sons most unlike Gods.
Divine ye were created, and divine
In sad demeanour, solemn, undisturb'd.
Unruffled, like high Gods, ye liv'd and ruled:
Now I behold in you fear, hope, and wrath;
Actions of rage and passion; even as
I see them, on the mortal world beneath,
In men who die.—This is the grief, O Son!
Sad sign of ruin, sudden dismay, and fall!
Yet do thou strive; as thou art capable,
As thou canst move about, an evident God;
And canst oppose to each malignant hour
Ethereal presence:—I am but a voice;
My life is but the life of winds and tides,
No more than winds and tides can I avail:—
But thou canst.—Be thou therefore in the van
Of circumstance; yea, seize the arrow's barb
Before the tense string murmur.—To the earth!
For there thou wilt find Saturn, and his woes.
Meantime I will keep watch on thy bright sun,
And of thy seasons be a careful nurse."—
Ere half this region-whisper had come down,
Hyperion arose, and on the stars
Lifted his curved lids, and kept them wide
Until it ceas'd; and still he kept them wide:
And still they were the same bright, patient stars.
Then with a slow incline of his broad breast,
Like to a diver in the pearly seas,
Forward he stoop'd over the airy shore,
And plung'd all noiseless into the deep night.

The greater part of Men make their way with the same instinctive-ness, the same unwandering eye from their purposes, the same animal eagerness as the Hawk—The Hawk wants a Mate, so does the Man—look at them both they set about it and procure on[e] in the same manner—They want both a nest and they both set about one in the same manner—they get their food in the same manner—The noble animal Man for his amusement smokes his pipe—the Hawk balances about the Clouds—that is the only difference of their leisures. This it is that makes the Amusement of Life—to a speculative Mind. I go among the Fields and catch a glimpse of a stoat or a fieldmouse peeping out of the withered grass—the creature hath a purpose and its eyes are bright with it—I go amongst the buildings of a city and I see a Man hurrying along—to what ? The Creature has a purpose and his eyes are bright with it. But then as Wordsworth says, "we have all one human heart"—there is an electric fire in human nature tending to purify—so that among these human creatures there is continually some birth of new heroism—The pity is that we must wonder at it: as we should at finding a pearl in rubbish—I have no doubt that thousands of people never heard of have had hearts comp[l]etely disinterested: I can remember but two—Socrates and Jesus—their Histories evince it. . . .

I myself am pursuing the same instinctive course as the veriest human animal you can think of—I am however young writing at random—straining at particles of light in the midst of a great darkness—without knowing the bearing of any one assertion of any one opinion. Yet may I not in this be free from sin ?

—To George and Georgiana Keats, March 19, 1819.

"THE VALE OF SOUL-MAKING"

The common cognomen of this world among the misguided and superstitious is 'a vale of tears' from which we are to be redeemed by a certain arbitrary interposition of God and taken to Heaven—What a little circumscribed straightened notion! Call the world if you Please "The vale of Soul-making" Then you will find out the use of the world (I am speaking now in the highest terms for human nature admitting it to be immortal which I will here take for granted for the purpose of showing a thought which has struck me concerning it) I say 'Soul making' Soul as distinguished from an Intelligence—There may be intelligences or sparks of the divinity in millions—but they are not Souls till they acquire identities, till each one is personally itself. Intelligences are atoms of perception—they know and they see and they are pure, in short they are God—how then are Souls to be made? How then are these sparks which are God to have identity given them—so as ever to possess a bliss peculiar to each one's individual existence? How, but by the medium of a world like this?

—To George and Georgiana Keats, April 21, 1819.

"THE MOST GENUINE BEING IN THE WORLD"

One of my Ambitions is to make as great a revolution in modern dramatic writing as Kean has done in acting—another to upset the drawling of the blue stocking literary world—if in the course of a few years I do these two things I ought to die content—and my friends should drink a dozen of Claret on my Tomb—I am convinced more and more every day that (excepting the human friend Philosopher) a fine writer is the most genuine Being in the World—Shakspeare and the Paradise Lost every day become greater wonders to me—I look upon fine Phrases like a Lover.

—To Benjamin Bailey, August 14, 1819.

FROM: THE FALL OF HYPERION

Canto One

FANATICS have their dreams, wherewith they weave
A paradise for a sect; the savage, too,
From forth the loftiest fashion of his sleep
Guesses at Heaven; pity these have not
Trac'd upon vellum or wild Indian leaf
The shadows of melodious utterance.
But bare of laurel they live, dream, and die;
For Poesy alone can tell her dreams,—
With the fine spell of words alone can save
Imagination from the sable chain
And dumb enchantment—Who alive can say,
"Thou art no Poet—may'st not tell thy dreams?"
Since every man whose soul is not a clod
Hath visions, and would speak, if he had lov'd,
And been well nurtured in his mother tongue.
Whether the dream now purpos'd to rehearse
Be poet's or fanatic's will be known
When this warm scribe, my hand, is in the grave.

Methought I stood where trees of every clime,
Palm, myrtle, oak, and sycamore, and beech,
With plantain, and spice-blossoms, made a screen;
In neighbourhood of fountains by the noise
Soft-showering in mine ears and by the touch
Of scent, not far from roses. Turning round
I saw an arbour with a drooping roof
Of trellis vines, and bells, and larger blooms,

Like floral censers, swinging light in air;
Before its wreathed doorway, on a mound
Of moss, was spread a feast of summer fruits,
Which, nearer seen, seem'd refuse of a meal
By angel tasted or our Mother Eve;
For empty shells were scatter'd on the grass,
And grape-stalks but half bare, and remnants more,
Sweet-smelling, whose pure kinds I could not know.
Still was more plenty than the fabled horn
Thrice emptied could pour forth, at banqueting
For Proserpine return'd to her own fields,
Where the white heifers low. And appetite,
More yearning than on earth I ever felt,
Growing within, I ate deliciously;
And, after not long, thirsted; for thereby
Stood a cool vessel of transparent juice,
Sipp'd by the wander'd bee, the which I took,
And, pledging all the mortals of the world,
And all the dead whose names are in our lips,
Drank. That full draught is parent of my theme.
No Asian poppy nor elixir fine
Of the soon-fading, jealous Caliphat,
No poison gender'd in close monkish cells,
To thin the scarlet conclave of old men,
Could so have rapt unwilling life away.
Among the fragrant husks and berries crush'd
Upon the grass, I struggled hard against
The domineering potion, but in vain.
The cloudy swoon came on, and down I sunk,
Like a Silenus on an antique vase.
How long I slumbered 'tis a chance to guess.
When sense of life return'd, I started up
As if with wings, but the fair trees were gone,

The mossy mound and arbour were no more:
I look'd around upon the carved sides
Of an old sanctuary with roof august,
Builded so high, it seem'd that filmed clouds
Might spread beneath, as o'er the stars of heaven.
So old the place was, I remember'd none
The like upon the earth: what I had seen
Of gray cathedrals, buttress'd walls, rent towers,
The superannuations of sunk realms,
Or Nature's rocks toil'd hard in waves and winds,
Seem'd but the faulture of decrepit things
To that eternal domed monument.
Upon the marble at my feet there lay
Store of strange vessels, and large draperies,
Which needs had been of dyed asbestos wove,
Or in that place the moth could not corrupt,
So white the linen, so, in some, distinct
Ran imageries from a sombre loom.
All in a mingled heap confus'd there lay
Robes, golden tongs, censer and chafing-dish,
Girdles, and chains, and holy jewelries.

Turning from these with awe, once more I rais'd
My eyes to fathom the space every way;
The embossed roof, the silent massy range
Of columns north and south, ending in mist
Of nothing; then to eastward, where black gates
Were shut against the sunrise evermore.
Then to the west I look'd, and saw far off
An image, huge of feature as a cloud,
At level of whose feet an altar slept,
To be approach'd on either side by steps
And marble balustrade, and patient travail

To count with toil the innumerable degrees.
Towards the altar sober-pac'd I went,
Repressing haste, as too unholy there;
And, coming nearer, saw beside the shrine
One minist'ring; and there arose a flame.
When in mid-day the sickening east-wind
Shifts sudden to the south, the small warm rain
Melts out the frozen incense from all flowers,
And fills the air with so much pleasant health
That even the dying man forgets his shroud;—
Even so that lofty sacrificial fire,
Sending forth Maian incense, spread around
Forgetfulness of everything but bliss,
And clouded all the altar with soft smoke;
From whose white fragrant curtains thus I heard
Language pronounc'd: "If thou canst not ascend
These steps, die on that marble where thou art.
Thy flesh, near cousin to the common dust,
Will parch for lack of nutriment,—thy bones
Will wither in few years, and vanish so
That not the quickest eye could find a grain
Of what thou now art on that pavement cold.
The sands of thy short life are spent this hour,
And no hand in the universe can turn
Thy hourglass, if these gummed leaves be burnt
Ere thou canst mount up these immortal steps."

. . . . .

"Are there not thousands in the world," said I,
Encourag'd by the sooth voice of the shade,
"Who love their fellows even to the death;
Who feel the giant agony of the world;
And more, like slaves to poor humanity,
Labour for mortal good? I sure should see

Other men here, but I am here alone."
"Those whom thou spak'st of are no visionaries,"
Rejoin'd that voice,—"they are no dreamers weak;
They seek no wonder but the human face,
No music but a happy-noted voice—
They come not here, they have no thought to come—
And thou art here, for thou art less than they.
What benefit canst thou do, or all thy tribe,
To the great world? Thou art a dreaming thing,
A fever of thy self—think of the earth;
What bliss, even in hope, is there for thee?
What haven? every creature hath its home;
Every sole man hath days of joy and pain,
Whether his labours be sublime or low—
The pain alone, the joy alone, distinct:
Only the dreamer venoms all his days,
Bearing more woe than all his sins deserve.
Therefore, that happiness be somewhat shar'd,
Such things as thou art are admitted oft
Into like gardens thou didst pass erewhile,
And suffer'd in these temples: for that cause
Thou standest safe beneath this statue's knees."
"That I am favour'd for unworthiness,
By such propitious parley medicin'd
In sickness not ignoble, I rejoice,
Aye, and could weep for love of such award."
So answer'd I, continuing, "If it please,
Majestic shadow, tell me: sure not all
Those melodies sung into the world's ear
Are useless: sure a poet is a sage;
A humanist, physician to all men.
That I am none I feel, as vultures feel
They are no birds when eagles are abroad.

What am I then: thou spakest of my tribe:
What tribe?" The tall shade veil'd in drooping white
Then spake, so much more earnest, that the breath
Moved the thin linen folds that drooping hung
About a golden censer from the hand
Pendent—"Art thou not of the dreamer tribe?
The poet and the dreamer are distinct,
Diverse, sheer opposite, antipodes.
The one pours out a balm upon the world,
The other vexes it."

                    .   .   .   .   .
. . . . No stir of life
Was in this shrouded vale, not so much air
As in the zoning of a summer's day
Robs not one light seed from the feather'd grass;
But where the dead leaf fell, there did it rest:
A stream went voiceless by, still deaden'd more
By reason of the fallen Divinity
Spreading more shade; the Naiad 'mid her reeds
Press'd her cold finger closer to her lips.

    Along the margin sand large footmarks went
No farther than to where old Saturn's feet
Had rested, and there slept, how long a sleep!
Degraded, cold, upon the sodden ground
His old right hand lay nerveless, listless, dead,
Unsceptred, and his realmless eyes were clos'd;
While his bow'd head seem'd listening to the Earth,
His antient mother, for some comfort yet.

I have given up Hyperion—there were too many Miltonic inversions in it—Miltonic verse cannot be written but in an artful or rather artist's humour. I wish to give myself up to other sensations. English ought to be kept up. It may be interesting to you to pick out some lines from Hyperion and put a mark X to the false beauty proceeding from art, and one || to the true voice of feeling.

—To J. H. Reynolds, September 21, 1819.

VIII. Love and Death

FIRST MEETING

Shall I give you Miss Brawn[e] ? She is about my height—with a fine style of countenance of the lengthen'd sort—she wants sentiment in every feature—she manages to make her hair look well—her nostrills are fine—though a little painful—her mouth is bad and good—her Profil is better than her full-face which indeed is not full but pale and thin without showing any bone—Her shape is very graceful and so are her movements—her Arms are good her hands badish—her feet tolerable —she is not seventeen—but she is ignorant—monstrous in her behaviour flying out in all directions, calling people such names—that I was forced lately to make use of the term Minx—*this is I think not from any innate vice but from a penchant she has for acting stylishly.*

— To George and Georgiana Keats, December 18, 1818.

FROM THE LETTERS TO FANNY BRAWNE

I.

Why may I not speak of your Beauty, since without that I could never have lov'd you—I cannot conceive any beginning of such love as I have for you but Beauty. There may be a sort of love for which, without the least sneer at it, I have the highest respect, and can admire it in others: but it has not the richness, the bloom, the full form, the enchantment of love after my own heart. So let me speak of your Beauty, though to my own endangering; if you could be so cruel to me as to try elsewhere its Power. You say you are afraid I shall think you do not love me—in saying this you make me ache the more to be near you. I am at the diligent use of my faculties here, I do not pass a day without sprawling some blank verse or tagging some rhymes; and here I must confess, that, (since I am on that subject,) I love you the more in that I believe you have liked me for my own sake and for nothing else—I have met with women whom I really think would like to be married to a Poem and to be given away by a Novel.

—July 8, 1819.

Forgive me if I wander a little this evening, for I have been all day employ'd in a very abstract Poem and I am in deep love with you—two things which must excuse me. I have, believe me, not been an age in letting you take possession of me; the very first week I knew you I wrote myself your vassal; but burnt the Letter as the very next time I saw you I thought you manifested some dislike to me. If you should ever feel for Man at the first sight what I did for you, I am lost. Yet I should not quarrel with you, but hate myself if such a thing were to happen—only I should burst if the thing were not as fine as a Man as you are as a Woman. Perhaps I am too vehement, then fancy me on my knees, especially when I mention a part of your Letter which hurt me; you say speaking of Mr. Severn "but you must be satisfied in knowing that I admired you much more than your friend." My dear love, I cannot believe there ever was or ever could be any thing to admire in me especially as far as sight goes—I cannot be admired, I am not a thing to be admired. You are, I love you; all I can bring you is a swooning admiration of your Beauty. I hold that place among Men which snubnos'd brunettes with meeting eyebrows do among women—they are trash to me—unless I should find one among them with a fire in her heart like the one that burns in mine. You absorb me in spite of myself— you alone: for I look not forward with any pleasure to what is call'd being settled in the world; I tremble at domestic cares—yet for you I would meet them, though if it would leave you the happier I would rather die than do so. I have two luxuries to brood over in my walks, your Loveliness and the hour of my death. O that I could have possession of them both in the same minute.

—July 25, 1819.

3

The time is passed when I had power to advise and warn you against the unpromising morning of my Life—My love has made me selfish. I cannot exist without you—I am forgetful of every thing but seeing you again—my Life seems to stop there—I see no further. You have absorb'd me. I have a sensation at the present moment as though I was dissolving—I should be exquisitely miserable without the hope of soon seeing you. I should be afraid to separate myself far from you. My sweet Fanny, will your heart never change? My love, will it? I have no limit now to my love—Your note came in just here—I cannot be happier away from you—'Tis richer than an Argosy of Pearles. Do not threat me even in jest. I have been astonished that Men could die Martyrs for religion—I have shudder'd at it—I shudder no more—I could be martyr'd for my Religion—Love is my religion—I could die for that—I could die for you. My Creed is Love and you are its only tenet—You have ravish'd me away by a Power I cannot resist; and yet I could resist till I saw you; and even since I have seen you I have endeavoured often "to reason against the reasons of my Love." I can do that no more—the pain would be too great—My Love is selfish—I cannot breathe without you.

—*October 13, 1819.*

4.

How illness stands as a barrier betwixt me and you! Even if I was well——I must make myself as good a Philosopher as possible. Now I have had opportunities of passing nights anxious and awake I have found other thoughts intrude upon me. "If I should die," said I to myself, "I have left no immortal work behind me—nothing to make my friends proud of my memory—but I have lov'd the principle of beauty in all things, and if I had had time I would have made myself remember'd."

—*February (?), 1820.*

WHY DID I LAUGH

Why did I laugh to-night? No voice will tell:
  No God, no Demon of severe response,
Deigns to reply from heaven or from Hell.
  Then to my human heart I turn at once.
Heart! Thou and I are here sad and alone;
  Say, wherefore did I laugh? O mortal pain!
O Darkness! Darkness! ever must I moan,
  To question Heaven and Hell and Heart in vain.
Why did I laugh? I know this Being's lease,
  My fancy to its utmost blisses spreads;
Yet would I on this very midnight cease,
  And the world's gaudy ensigns see in shreds;
Verse, Fame, and Beauty are intense indeed,
But Death intenser—Death is Life's high meed.

TO SLEEP

O soft embalmer of the still midnight,
  Shutting, with careful fingers and benign,
Our gloom-pleas'd eyes, embower'd from the light,
  Enshaded in forgetfulness divine;
O soothest Sleep! if so it please thee, close
  In midst of this thine hymn, my willing eyes,
Or wait the Amen, ere thy poppy throws
  Around my bed its lulling charities;
Then save me, or the passed day will shine
Upon my pillow, breeding many woes;
  Save me from curious conscience, that still lords
Its strength for darkness, burrowing like a mole;
  Turn the key deftly in the oiled wards,
And seal the hushed casket of my soul.

BRIGHT STAR

BRIGHT STAR, would I were steadfast as thou art—
  Not in lone splendour hung aloft the night
And watching, with eternal lids apart,
  Like nature's patient, sleepless Eremite,
The moving waters at their priestlike task
  Of pure ablution round earth's human shores,
Or gazing on the new soft fallen mask
  Of snow upon the mountains and the moors—
No—yet still steadfast, still unchangeable,
  Pillow'd upon my fair love's ripening breast,
To feel for ever its soft fall and swell,
  Awake for ever in a sweet unrest,
Still, still to hear her tender-taken breath,
And so live ever—or else swoon to death.

TO FANNY

I CRY YOUR MERCY—pity—love!—aye, love!
 Merciful love that tantalizes not,
One-thoughted, never-wandering, guileless love,
 Unmask'd, and being seen—without a blot!
O! let me have thee whole,—all—all—be mine!
 That shape, that fairness, that sweet minor zest
Of love, your kiss,—those hands, those eyes divine,
 That warm, white, lucent, million-pleasured breast,—
Yourself—your soul—in pity give me all,
 Withhold no atom's atom or I die,
Or living on perhaps, your wretched thrall,
 Forget, in the mist of idle misery,
 Life's purposes,—the palate of my mind
Losing its gust, and my ambition blind!

THE DAY IS GONE

THE DAY IS GONE, and all its sweets are gone!
  Sweet voice, sweet lips, soft hand, and softer breast,
Warm breath, light whisper, tender semi-tone,
  Bright eyes, accomplish'd shape, and lang'rous waist!
Faded the flower and all its budded charms,
  Faded the sight of beauty from my eyes,
Faded the shape of beauty from my arms,
  Faded the voice, warmth, whiteness, paradise—
Vanish'd unseasonably at shut of eve,
  When the dusk holiday—or holinight
Of fragrant-curtain'd love begins to weave
  The woof of darkness thick, for hid delight;
But, as I've read love's missal through to-day,
He'll let me sleep, seeing I fast and pray.

LINES SUPPOSED TO HAVE BEEN ADDRESSED
TO FANNY BRAWNE

THIS LIVING HAND, now warm and capable
Of earnest grasping, would, if it were cold
And in the icy silence of the tomb,
So haunt thy days and chill thy dreaming nights
That thou would[st] wish thine own heart dry of blood
So in my veins red life might stream again,
And thou be conscience-calm'd—see here it is—
I hold it towards you.

INDEX OF FIRST LINES

INDEX OF TITLES

ABOUT THE COMPILER

Stanley Kunitz was awarded the 1959 Pulitzer Prize in poetry for his *Selected Poems*, his third book of verse, which confirmed his reputation as one of America's best poets. As editor and biographer, he is responsible for *Twentieth Century Authors* and other standard works of literary reference. As critic, he writes on literature and the fine arts for the leading contemporary journals.

Born in Worcester, Massachusetts, Mr. Kunitz was educated at Harvard University and received an honorary Litt.D. from Clark University. For several years he edited the *Wilson Library Bulletin*. The colleges at which he has taught include Bennington, The New School, The University of Washington, and Brandeis; currently he lectures at Columbia University. In addition he has visited numerous American colleges as Danforth Visiting Lecturer and as a reader of his own poetry.

His many other honors include a Guggenheim Fellowship, a Ford Foundation grant, the Amy Lowell Poetry Travelling Fellowship, *Poetry*'s Levinson Prize, and the Harriet Monroe Award given by the University of Chicago. He is a member of the National Institute of Arts & Letters.

ABOUT THE ARTIST

Jacques Hnizdovsky, a well-known graphic artist, was born in the Ukraine and studied art in Warsaw and in Zagreb. In 1949, Mr. Hnizdovsky emigrated to the United States and became a naturalized citizen in 1954.

He is represented in the permanent collections of the Museum of Fine Arts in Boston, the Library of Congress, the U. S. Information Service and several other museums throughout this country. Mr. Hnizdovsky now lives in New York, with his wife and young daughter.